10.02
12/91

THE GIFT

Hilda Doolittle with her brothers, Harold and Gilbert

The Gift

H.D.

A NEW DIRECTIONS BOOK

57038

The publisher gratefully acknowledges the co-operation of the Collection
of American Literature of the Beinecke Rare Book & Manuscript Library
of Yale University for making the manuscript as well as the photographs
of H.D. and of her mother available.

The chapter "The Dream" was first published in *Contemporary Literature*.

Manufactured in the United States of America
First published clothbound and as New Directions Paperbook 546 in 1982.
Published simultaneously in Canada by George J. McLeod, Toronto.

Library of Congress Cataloging in Publication Data

H. D. (Hilda Doolittle), 1886–1961.
  The gift.
  (A New Directions Book)
  I. Title.
PS3507.0726G5   1982   813'.52   82-8207
ISBN 0-8112-0853-2   AACR2
ISBN 0-8112-0854-0 (pbk.)

New Directions Books are published for James Laughlin
by New Directions Publishing Corp.
80 Eighth Avenue, New York 10011.

To
HELEN
who has
brought me home
for Bethlehem Pennsylvania 1741
from Chelsea London 1941

L'amitié passe même le tombeau

UNLESS A BOMB FALLS . . .

"Morning coffee, lunches and teas as usual unless a bomb falls on the building." So read the notice at H. D.'s local restaurant, The Tea Kettle. Then, one morning: "more open than usual." The waitresses were still sweeping up broken glass. And they were very apologetic. "Sorry, only cold cuts and salad today, we seem to have lost our gas main." They provided good scalding tea, however—brewed on a camping stove. Life had to go on, and so it did; cheerfully and sometimes grumpily—unless and until a bomb fell on the building.

Bryher had moved into H. D.'s apartment—close quarters for two such turbulent spirits. To accommodate the material overflow she rented storage space in the basement. When the raids intensified, she hauled in two lumpy mattresses and created a private shelter. There they spent many noisy nights. As soon as the All Clear wailed, they went back upstairs, breakfasted, and started the working day.

Bryher was the housekeeper and provider; off early, heading every queue. She left the house with a clutch of empty string bags, and always managed to fill them. She returned laden like a pack pony. Then she went to her chaotic room— papers strewn all over the bed and under it, typewriter teetering atop a spindly tea table—and attended to her correspondence; average, twenty letters a day. She also wrote a novel based on the management and clientele of The Tea Kettle. And started another about the Battle of Hastings. With the door open, the telephone ringing, and Mrs. Ash the charlady mopping, and popping in for chats.

H. D. needed structure, total privacy, and the strictest schedule. Notebooks laid out in neat piles, pencils sharpened the night before. Everything ready, set to go—unless a bomb fell on the building. She got a good headstart while Bryher was off on her rounds, and finished before Mrs. Ash came. Two, three hours at the most. Every day, seven days a week. "Just going over some old stuff," she said. "I don't expect anything to come of it, but it's healing to the psyche." She volunteered no more, and I certainly wasn't going to inquire. "When I talk about my work," she once told me "it skids and shatters and gets away." To this day, I never ask a writer what he or she is "doing."

Normally a voracious reader and eternal student, she now found it hard to concentrate on her beloved books. There was plenty of time in the afternoons and during the long evenings, but the times were "disintegrating"—one of her key words. Her psyche refused to lose itself in the printed page. So she turned to needlework. It kept her hands busy and freed her mind to soar or to settle, to enjoy BBC concerts, to converse with her friends. She kept it in a floppy brown bag along with the wool—lovely soft skeins of every shade. She always brought it out after tea, and worked away while guests lingered on. When they left, she continued till dinner time. She completed an elaborate masterpiece which hangs on my wall. Strange hybrid animals prowl an overladen fruit grove. She started another. I have that too—same bag, same wool, undamaged by time or moth. I will finish it for her some day.

We were together one evening, just the two of us. She was stitching, lost in thought. I was reading. Bryher burst in on the peaceful scene to announce that the apple jelly had exploded and ruined her books. For some unexplained reason, she kept supplies in the back of her bookcase. A jar had leaked. Drama, consternation. A very special jar, Fortnum & Mason, prewar apple jelly, which she was saving for Edith Sitwell. Would it do? We sampled it on the spot. It had crystallized on top and turned runny at the bottom, and fermented; it was really quite nasty throughout. Edith would have to settle for black currant, as yet intact.

The incident triggered H. D.'s memory. Other apples, the orchards of Pennsylvania, the woods she wandered with her brothers Alfred and Eric. "Brothers . . . ?" I interrupted. I knew Harold and Melvin; I knew of Gilbert, killed in the First World War. Here were two new uncles. Why had they never been mentioned? Were they undesirables, black sheep of some kind—or illegitimate? I was quite indignant.

"Only half brothers. My father's first wife died and he married her sister."

"You never *told* me—"

"Oh well, it was all so long ago and there seemed no point in bringing it up."

Long ago and far away and enough reminiscence for the day. I left it at that. She never revealed much about her early background; she merely dropped bits of information now and then. My father was out of the picture, so my relatives were all on my mother's side—and on the other side of the world, the States. A few of them came over. Uncle Harold and Uncle Melvin. And my grandmother and her sister, my great-aunt Laura, whom I loved dearly. They baby-sat when Bryher and H. D. traveled. But they both returned to the States when I was still a young child. Aunt Laura outlived my grandmother by a few years. I never saw either of them again.

My late grandfather sounded awesome. An astronomer. I visualized him as a bearded sage, like Copernicus in *The Child's Book of the Heavens.*

Now, as I read *The Gift* I see that I wasn't far wrong. Professor Charles Doolittle was "a path-finder, an explorer" so intent on his work that he literally froze to the telescope. His beard and whiskers had to be thawed out at regular intervals. The household revolved around him, especially the women. Everybody was understandably traumatized when he staggered home late one night, incoherent, bruised, and smeared with blood. Little Hilda never recovered from the shock, nor is the mystery explained within the context of the book. A letter was discovered recently. It appears that the Professor stepped off a moving trolley. Maybe he forgot to press the stop button, maybe the driver didn't hear it. The passenger stepped off into space and took a nasty tumble. Anyway, he survived. His loved ones rallied and bandaged him and nursed him back to health.

Although he was a genius and a dominant figure, he seems to have been a man of great personal warmth. He cared deeply about his family and observed all the traditions—Christmas and birthday celebrations, summer excursions to huts and parks and lakes.

It was an extensive family. Five sons and a daughter, uncles and aunts and cousins, and old grandmother Mamalie. A distinguished family too.

Mamalie's father, Grandpa Weiss, was a superlative clockmaker. He also played the trombone, and kept bees. We have inherited one of his clocks. It has traveled far—down through the generations, down to the Southern Hemisphere, following Uncle Melvin to his post in Buenos Aires; and back to New York and out to Long Island. A local artisan rebuilt it for us; he was greatly impressed by the beauty and craftsmanship. Outwardly, it has recovered from its sea changes. But we are chary of its mechanism and delicate balance, and unable to give it the full time attention it requires. So it stands in our parlor, a friendly silent presence, set at 7:15.

Uncle Fred was put to work in a drugstore—a singularly inept choice of career. All he cared about was music. Yes, they finally admitted, he had artistic gift. They let him follow his true vocation. He later founded the Bach Choir, and the famous Bach Festival, still an annual event in Bethlehem.

Mama—my grandmother—had a talent for painting. She was musical too; she sang in the choir. A fortune-teller predicted that she would have a child who was exceptionally gifted. She withdrew from the competition. She never painted or sang again.

The gifted child was, of course, Hilda. Little Hilda, who had no inkling of it for many years to come. The book is written entirely from a child's point of view.

Where did the Gift come from? Was it in the air? Or inherited? Where did it originate? Probably with Mamalie, whose gift was weird—psychic recall. She could remember things that happened before she was born. Maybe she was a frustrated historical novelist who talked her books. The present was a jumble. She mixed up names and faces, current dates, places. She confused Hilda with Cousin Aggie. The child ignored the mistake and curled up for a late night chat which turned into a lengthy seance. Hilda/Aggie was mesmerized. She knew she had to keep the old lady talking; otherwise she would go to sleep and never finish the story. Worse still, she might lapse into German, the incomprehensible language of her forebears. Already, she was dropping words like *Gnadenhuetten,* and *Wunden Eiland.*

The first Moravians settled in eastern Pennsylvania, probably welcomed by the Quakers, who were more tolerant than New England Protestants or Southern Catholic states. These early worshipers came from England, the Low Countries, and various parts of Germany. They took refuge on Count Zinsendorff's estate in Moravia. He organized their transatlantic journey. Thus a polyglot group founded Bethlehem. The language spoken was a species of German, the tongue of the majority.

The Moravians are not to be confused with the Amish or other Pennsylvania Dutch sects, from whom they differed by having a livelier interest in learning and culture. Music was an essential part of their lives. Many of the Moravians were skilled artisans. Their work is evident in the church and academy buildings of Bethlehem.

Their belief was a literal following of the Bible, and they were especially peace-loving. They soon made friends with the Indians, many of whom they converted, even to the extent of turning nomadic warlike tribes into peaceful tillers of the soil like themselves.

They devised an original and enchanting method of communication in those pretelephone days. A quartet of trombonists gathered on a balcony atop the church tower, facing the four points of the compass. The changes they played were familiar to all. One heralded a birth, one sounded an alarm, another a death—and so on. Every citizen, musical or not, was trained to interpret the notes drifting out over the town and countryside from those golden horns.

Wunden Eiland—Isle of Wounds. There must have been occasional dissensions, tribal clashes, and confrontations.

Mamalie rambled on, further and further into the past. The child couldn't take it all in. She pieced it together, later. She became aware of "the Thing"—synonymous with the Gift—atavism, transmigration of souls, the weight of past events. She couldn't understand it. She felt haunted, trapped within it. Never free until "again there was a whistling of evil wings, the falling of poisonous arrows, the deadly signature of a sign of evil magic in the sky." The London Blitz, that unreal—and all too real—time, which she describes in the final chapter, or epilogue. When writing was her therapy. Some of it was wrought from direct experience:

> *An incident here and there,*
> *and rails gone (for guns)*
> *from your (and my) old town square*

The Gift provided escape. Her mind was obviously deep into it and far away, on the afternoon of the exploding apple jelly.

The original manuscript of *The Gift* was much longer. Judicious cutting has not affected the spirit, or the quality, but has made a better book.

Forty years have passed since *The Gift* was written. The Gift continues on, following its own course. It can't be pushed or pulled. I ponder my oldest son's interest in astrophysics, his way with the written word, and his great appreciation of music. His three siblings are also "into" literature and the arts. Their musical tastes might seem eclectic, but it's all part of the whole. I'm sure Uncle Fred would have loved the Beatles.

On September 10th, H. D.'s birthday, we travel to Bethlehem. Hospitable friends have entertained us there over the years, always after funerals. We now meet annually, to celebrate a happy occasion. There is a reading, and a tea, and a twilight procession to Nisky Hill Cemetery. We lay flowers alongside the beautiful inscription—"Greek flower; Greek ecstasy. . . ."—saving some for the other Doolittles and Wolles. Professor Charles Doolittle and my grandmother and Aunt Laura. And Uncle Gilbert and Uncle Fred. All weathered and mossy, barely legible. And Uncle Harold, Uncle Melvin, and Aunt Dorothy—shiny new by comparison.

Just beyond this enclave there is a stone book, half open, and anonymous; the pages are blank. An innocent's grave, maybe. A baby, or a fragile young girl, whose life was an open book. Or a renegade whose story could not be told. A venerable scholar—or a poet. The Gift, in another family.

PERDITA SCHAFFNER

THE GIFT

The brain comes into play, yes, but it is only
the tool. . . . the telephone is not the person speaking
over it. The dark room is not the photograph.

Death and its Mystery, Camille Flammarion

⁂ DARK ROOM

There was a girl who was burnt to death at the seminary, as they called the old school where our grandfather was principal.

For a long time we were under the impression that we had two fathers, Papa and Papalie, but the children across the street said Papalie was our grandfather. "He is not," we said, "he is our Papalie." But Ida, our devoted friend, who did the cooking and read Grimm's tales to us at night before we went to sleep, said yes, Papalie was our grandfather, people had a grandfather, sometimes they had two. The other grandfather was dead, he was Papa's father, she explained. But the girl who was burnt to death, was burnt to death in a crinoline. The Christmas tree was lighted at the end of one of the long halls and the girl's ruffles or ribbons caught fire and she was in a great hoop.

The other girls stand round. There is Mama, who is a tiny child, and Aunt Laura, who Mama said was the pretty one, two years older, and Aunt Agnes in her long frock, who in the daguerreotypes and old photographs looked like the young mother of the two little girls and the three boys, the uncles.

Mamalie had married twice; there was a picture of one of Aunt Agnes' family in a wig with a sword; he had been at the Court of Czar Alexander, in Russia; that was a long time ago. Aunt Agnes' children were young men, almost like uncles. There had been eight altogether; five grew up. There had been a little girl; and in our own plot at Nisky Hill, there was a little girl who was our own sister and another little girl who had been the child of the Lady who had been Papa's first wife. But the girl in the crinoline wasn't a relation, she was just one of the many girls at the seminary when Papalie was there and she screamed and Papalie rushed to her and Papalie wrapped a rug around her, but she is shrieking and they can not tear off her clothes because of the hoop.

"Why are you crying?" This is Mama and her younger brother, little Hartley. Mamalie finds them crouched at the turn of the stairs under the big clock that Mamalie's father had made himself.

"It is a grandfather clock," we said proudly, "and it was made by Mamalie's family."

"Ah, so it is *really* a grandfather's clock," one out-of-town visitor remarked; we felt indifference, even irreverence in her unfamiliar low drawl. Wasn't it a thing to be proud of, that Mamalie's father made clocks? We were very proud of it. Mamalie's father had even been asked to Philadelphia to sing in a great choral-service; he kept bees and he played the trombone at the Easter service in the old graveyard when we went out and said *the Lord is risen indeed* and watched the sun come up over the graves.

But "why are you crying" was Mama and little Hartley, it was not Hilda and little Harold. Hilda and little Harold did not creep under the clock and cry, but it was the same clock.

"Why are you crying?"

Mama, who was older, said, "We are crying because Fanny died." Mamalie laughed and told us the story of Mama and Uncle Hartley crouching under the clock, which was our clock in our house now and our great-grandfather had made it and kept bees and been asked to Philadelphia to sing, even at a theater or an opera house.

"They were crying," Mamalie explained, when we wondered why she laughed about it, "because Fanny died."

"But why is it funny?"

"Well, you see they couldn't possibly remember Fanny. Fanny died before Hartley was born, and your own mama was just a baby, how could she remember Fanny?"

I wondered about that. Mama was crying about Fanny. Why did Mamalie think it funny? Mamalie did not seem to think of Fanny, Mama did not speak often of little Edith, and the other little girl was not mentioned. Ida said it was better for us not to share Edith's flowers on her April birthday with the other graves, with the Lady, and with Alice. We felt somehow that this was not right, but there were things we did not understand.

We had spread Edith's pansies equally on Alice's twin grave and then borrowed from both of them for the Lady who was not our mother but the mother of the two (to us) grown men, our brothers, who were finishing their work at the university across the river; their names were Eric and Alfred. But Ida said the flowers were meant for Edith and "your mama would feel hurt." We did not follow this, but had been sent with the basket of pansies and pink-and-white button-daisies for Edith's grave, so we collected the pansies and daisies from the flat tops of the other graves and gave them back to Edith. And then there was Fanny, difficult to find in the crowded plot where Mamalie's and Aunt Agnes' other children were. There was Elizabeth Caroline for instance, who had been Aunt Agnes' and Uncle Will's first baby. But Fanny, among them all, had become a myth; she was a family by-word. "Why so sad, Helen?" Mamalie might say. Then Mama would answer, perhaps too suddenly, too swiftly, forcing the expected "Mimmie, of course, you know why. I'm crying because Fanny died." And they would both laugh.

I seemed to have inherited that. I was the inheritor. The boys, of whom there were so many—the two brothers and later the baby-brother, the two half-brothers, the five grown Howard cousins, not to mention the small-fry, Tootie, Dick and Laddie (who lived with their parents, our Uncle Hartley and Aunt Belle in the house next to ours, on Church Street)—could not really care about Fanny; little Hartley had cried only because his tiny older sister was crying. I cared about Fanny. And she died. I inherited Fanny from Mama, from Mamalie, if you will, but I inherited Fanny. Was I indeed, Frances come back? Then I would be Papalie's own child, for Papalie's name was Francis; I would be like Mama; in a sense, I would be Mama, I would have important sisters, and brothers only as seemly ballast. Why was it always a girl who had died? Why did Alice die and not Alfred? Why did Edith die and not Gilbert? I did not cry because Fanny died, but I had inherited Fanny. Mama cried (although I had seldom seen her cry) because Fanny died, so Mama had cried. I did not cry. The crying was frozen in me, but it was my own, it was my own crying. There was Alice— my own half-sister, Edith—my own sister, and I was the third of this trio, these three Fates, or maybe Fanny was the third. The gift was there, but the expression of the gift was somewhere else.

It lay buried in the ground; in older countries, fragments of marble were brought to life again after long years. On these altars, flowers had lain, wild pansies, mountain laurel, roses. So we placed, in their season, daisies, roses, and peonies on those altars in the old graveyard where the stones lay flat, or in the new graveyard where the more worldly-minded newcomers to our town erected columns, artificially broken, around which carved ivy clung. They walled off their own personal little plots with white stones or low iron railings with chains, for to those newcomers to our town, death was a personal and private matter, not like the first Moravians who rested, more or less in the order of their going, under small stones that lay, even and symmetrical, like dominoes on a green baize cloth.

There was Miss Helen at school. There was the Beaver Lesson; the chart of the Beaver was hung on the wall beside the black and white drawing of the Eskimo and the Eskimo snowhouse. The Eskimo lived in a snowhouse, rather like the ones we tried to build, though we never succeeded in rounding them off neatly or, if they were any size, getting the roof to stay on. There was Miss Helen. There was the map she cut out of brown paper and the offering of a camel of mine pasted on. We brought pictures, cut out from the advertisements at the backs of magazines; Miss Helen chose those suitable for her brown-paper map of Africa; she pasted the animal or the palm tree where it belonged on the map. There was an oasis which was, she said, an island in the desert.

There were the Egyptians who lived along the river. They built little houses to live in when they were dead. In these underground houses they piled up furniture, chairs, tables, boxes, jars, food even. Some wheat taken out of a tomb (it had been buried thousands of years) grew when it was planted. The grain grew like the kernels of yellow corn we laid on a piece of mosquito-netting tied over a kitchen tumbler. We broke off the bare twigs of the chestnut trees, and the leaves came out, long before any green showed on the branches. The trees outside lined the brick walk that led up the slope from Church Street past the church and the dead-house (as we called the mortuary) to the school.

Florence said one of the Sisters was lying in the dead-house, but we could not see her. The dead-house had little windows, too high up, but Florence said Melinda had said that Nettie had said there was a Sister in the dead-house. She would lie there until they carried her to the old graveyard or more likely to Nisky Hill, as the old graveyard was very crowded. Along the fence of the old graveyard, there were mounds without stones, which were the soldiers, grey and blue, who had died in the old seminary when Papalie was there, during the Civil War. They were being taken in wagons to Philadelphia to the hospitals, but if they were too weak or going to die, they were left in the seminary on Church Street where they lay in rows in the beds where the girls had been, before they broke up the school to make a hospital of it for the soldiers from Gettysburg. There had been wounded soldiers there too, during the War of Independence.

Papa had been a soldier and Florence's father, too. Papa was only seventeen; he told them he was eighteen. He and his brother Alvin had gone off, and Alvin had died of typhoid fever. Papa had had typhoid, too. He said his mother cried when she saw him come back; she said, "Oh, I thought it was Alvin, coming back." Papa never told us much about himself except that his mother had been disappointed when she found it was Charles and not Alvin who had come back from the Civil War.

Papa went out to look at the stars at night. He measured them or measured something, we didn't know quite what. We could see what Papalie was doing with his microscope on his study table. But when Papa took us into his little domed house—with a dome like the Eskimo made of ice over their snow huts—and we asked to look into his telescope, he said that we would see nothing; you could not see what he was looking at, or looking for, in the daytime. Papa looked at a thermometer and opened or closed a shutter (that opened with ropes that pulled) in the curved roof or dome of his little house, which was built higher up the mountains, above the university buildings, the other side of the river. When we kept on asking him to let us see, he did let us see, but it was as he had told us; there was only a white glare and nothing to be seen and it hurt your eyes. It would be too late to go over there at night, he said, and anyhow, at night he was busy.

I can not say that a story called *Bluebeard* that Ida read us from one of the fairy tales, actually linked up in thought—how could it?—with our kind father. There was a man called *Bluebeard,* and he murdered his wives. How was it that Edith and Alice and the Lady (the mother of Alfred and Eric) all belonged to Papa and were there in the graveyard? No, of course, I did not actually put this two-and-two together.

"But why did they call him Bluebeard?" I asked Eric, who had time to answer questions that other people could not or would not answer. "His beard, was blue, was it?"

"No," said Eric, "it was just a way of saying that he had a very black beard."

Papa had a black beard. (A few years later, it was to turn white, almost overnight, but that comes later.) There was a man with a black beard and a dead wife or dead wives and there was Edith and there was Alice and there was the Lady whose name, written on stone, was, Ida told us ("but do not ask your mother questions"), Martha. The name Martha was written on a stone and Alice was written and

Edith. My name was Hilda; Papa found the name in the dictionary, he said. He said he ran his finger down the names in the back of the dictionary, and his finger stopped at Huldah and then went back up the line to Hilda. What would I have been, who would I have been, if my initial had come at the beginning and he had put his finger on Alice? Had he put his finger on Alice?

Papa went out of the house "like a thief" as he used to say, "or an astronomer," every evening if the stars were shining. If the stars were shining—O God of stars, let the stars shine—then Mama would lift the lamp from the center round-table in the sitting room and fold up the embroidered table-cover and say to Gilbert or Harold or Hilda, "Just take this pile of books, don't drop them, and put them on the piano; no, the piano is open, you can't reach up, not the floor, you don't put books on the floor, no, not the chair—here" and she would take them back and pile them on top of other books on the bookcase in the corner.

There was the cuckoo clock that would strike (too soon) eight, to-bed. There was the desk in the corner, in one of the compartments of which there was a little box with some sort of eggs, we were not sure what kind of eggs, "But they won't hatch now," Papalie had said. Mama thought they might be dangerous, be snake's eggs.

"But if they won't hatch, Mama, why don't you throw them away?"

"Oh—give me that box, I told you not to touch that box."

"But you said, Papalie said, they wouldn't hatch, can't I throw them in the garden?"

"No—no."

"Why not?"

"They might hatch."

"I thought you said, Papalie said, they wouldn't hatch now."

"He said, he *thought* they wouldn't hatch now."

"Then they might hatch—they might hatch here in the desk?"

"No, no, no—put that box down. Don't shake it."

"But I thought you said . . ."

Papalie had an alligator in their attic, in a tank with thick netting, but anyhow, "you children must not go up there any more."

"But the alligator is asleep."

Mamalie would tell us how someone who knew Papalie had sent him two alligators, as small as very large lizards, in a cigar box from Florida. They were wrapped in Florida moss. Their names were Castor and Pollux; one had died and was varnished and mounted on a board and hung over the slippery horsehair sofa in Papalie's study. Once a tarantula had dropped out of a bunch of bananas at Mr. Luckenbach's, the grocer on the corner.

Mr. Luckenbach had caught it in a shoe box and rushed across the street to ask Papalie what it was. Everyone brought things like that to our grandfather, because he had a microscope and studied things and drew pictures of branches of moss that you could not see with your eyes. He put them on a glass slide or pressed a drop of water from a bottle (that he had brought back from trips to the mountains) between two glass slides. That (in time, it was explained) was fresh-water *algae,* a sort of moss, invisible (for the most part) to the naked eye. The apple of my eye. He was the naked eye, he was the apple of God's eye. He was a minister, he read things out of the Bible, he said *I am the light of the world* when the doors opened at the far end of the church and the trays of lighted beeswax candles were brought into the church by the Sisters in their caps and aprons, while Uncle Fred in the gallery, at the organ was playing very softly *Holy Night*.

When Mama folded the embroidered table-cover and put it on top of the books, she might get out the jack-straws or she might get out of a box with a horseshoe that was a magnet and drew little bits of specks of iron in patterns after it. But she might turn over the cardboard box of yellow squares and say, "We will have some anagrams; Gilbert, you must help now."

There was not one single word that I could spell, not one, not c–a–t even, but if I shouldered over to Gilbert and clutched the edge of the table, I could from time to time select a letter; sometimes it was the right one, not very often.

"Mimmie, he's spelt a word," says Mama very proudly to Mamalie, our grandmother, or if it's Aunt Jennie, "Jean, look he's spelt dog," but Jean will push it back and say, "d–a–g doesn't spell anything that I know of; Sister would know an *a* from an *o* if you don't, Gibbie," and it might even be perceived that miraculously, a round shape in black, on the yellow square of cardboard, was somehow alone and staring at me, by Aunt Jennie's elbow.

It was a game, it was a way of making words out of words, but what it was was a way of spelling words, in fact it was a *spell*. The cuckoo clock would not strike; it could not, because the world had stopped. It was not frozen in time, it was like one of Papalie's water-drops that he had brought down from the mountains or from a trip to the Delaware Water Gap, in a jar. It was a drop of living and eternal life, perfected there; it was living, complete, not to be dried up in memory like pressed moss—Papalie had pressed moss, too. But there was a difference between Papalie's pressed moss and the things that shone in the crystal lens of his microscope, on the glass plate that a moment ago had been empty and just two pieces of glass, like small empty magic lantern slides, stuck together.

When Papalie lifted us, one by one in turn, to kneel on the chair by his worktable, we saw that it was true what he said, we saw that where there is nothing, there is something. We saw that an empty drop of water spread out branches, bright green or vermillion, in shape like a branch of a Christmas tree or in shape like a squashed peony or in shape like a lot of little green-glass beads, strung on a thick stem.

They had so much to give us, Papa and Papalie and old Father Weiss, as the whole town had affectionately called our grandmother's father. There were the others before these, who went back to the beginning of America and before America, but . . . we were none of us "gifted," they would say.

"How do you mean—what?"

"Oh—I don't mean—I don't mean anything."

But they did mean something. They didn't think any of us were marked with that strange thing they called a gift, the thing Uncle Fred had had from the beginning, the thing Papalie (they said) wasn't sure about, so Uncle Fred was put in a drugstore. An errand-boy who crawls under the counter and hides there with stolen fragments of church music was not much good in a drugstore. So Papalie made sure of the gift that Uncle Fred had. We hadn't any gift to make sure about.

But where did he get the gift, just like that? Why didn't

Mama wait and teach us music like she did Uncle Fred when he was a little boy? Mama gave all her music to Uncle Fred, that is what she did. That is why we hadn't the gift, because it was Mama who started being the musician, and then she said she taught Uncle Fred; she gave it away, she gave the gift to Uncle Fred, she should have waited and given the gift to us. But there were other gifts, it seemed.

"What—what do you mean, Uncle Hartley?"

"People draw, if a person draws or writes a book or something like that; a gift isn't just music. Artists are people who are gifted."

"Is Uncle Fred an artist?"

"Well, yes, I suppose so. Yes, of course Fred is an artist."

"But an artist is someone with a paintbox and a big hat?"

"No, an artist is someone who—well—he can draw or paint or write a book or even do other things."

"Like what?"

"Well, I don't know—well—to be *artistic*—I suppose you might say your Aunt Belle was *artistic*."

"Then can ladies be just the same as men?"

"Just the same what?"

"I mean what you said—about writing a book?"

"Why, yes, ladies write books of course, lots of ladies write very good books."

"Like Louisa M. Alcott?"

"Yes, like Louisa Alcott and like Harriet Beecher Stowe."

"Who is that?"

"That's *Uncle Tom's Cabin,* you know, you saw the procession and the play, didn't you?"

We saw Uncle Tom. He sat on a bench before a wooden hut that was drawn in a cart. The wooden hut was his cabin, and they told us that the book was called *Uncle Tom's Cabin* and that the play we were going to be taken to see, in a real theater, on the other side of the river, was called *Uncle Tom's Cabin,* but it was the book that started it or it was the real story, in the beginning, that started it, because Uncle Tom was a real darkie on a real plantation, *Way down upon the Sewanee river.*

That was before the Civil War; that happened a long time ago when Papa was seventeen, though he told them he was eighteen, so that he could run away with his brother Alvin in Indiana and help free the slaves.

The slaves were roped together and they walked along tied together like that, in torn trousers and old shoes or no shoes, and a man with a big hat and a whip, slashed round them with the whip, but Ida said he wasn't really hurting them, only cracking with his whip like that to show how Simon Legree (that was his name) drove the poor slaves in the cotton fields, down in the south.

There was someone on the ice with a baby, but the baby, Ida said, was a doll, and the ice was not real because it was summer and it would have melted. But Eliza, I think it was, was pulled along with the ice on wheels, like Uncle Tom's cabin. Then there were some horses and donkeys; it was a sort of golden cart or it was a chariot like *Swing low, sweet chariot,* and there was an angel, only it was made of wood and gilded over like the things on the Christmas tree, and it had a wreath in its hands. It was stretching out its wings and it was holding the wreath over the head of Little Eva who was the most important thing in the procession.

There were real dogs pulling on straps, with collars round their necks. They were very big dogs. Ida said they were bloodhounds, they were to hunt the slaves, and the slaves went along and they sang songs out of Uncle Bob's songbook on the top of the piano. They sang *Massa's in the cold, cold ground* or they just hummed, and then Simon

Legree cracked his whip and they stopped singing. The bloodhounds would chase them through the woods—only now they weren't slaves any more.

"It's only a parade," Gilbert said, "they are as free as you are."

The darkies tied together were as free as I was because our father and our Uncle Alvin had fought in the Civil War and now we all had the same flag that Betsy Ross made in a house in Philadelphia, which we have a picture of in school, with the thirteen original States which are the thirteen stripes and all the other States which are the Stars. Our State, which is Pennsylvania, is one of the thirteen original States.

Once we had a procession, too; we all waved flags when we met other children from other schools. That was for 1492, I mean it was in 1892 which made four hundred years since Columbus discovered America.

We were Americans and so were the darkies who were tied together and so was Simon Legree and so was Little Eva. Little Eva died in a bed, we saw her die. It was a stage, Ida said. You call it the stage, and this was our first time at the theater. We knew it was a stage because we had our school entertainments on the stage in the big hall at school. Now Little Eva died and it was just as if she had died, but then she came back again in a long nightgown. Little Eva was not really dead at all. She was the same little girl with the long gold hair who was driven in the chariot down the street, and she would do it all over again in Allentown or Easton, Ida said. They went on to other towns like the circus did, but this was not the circus. Uncle Tom died too, and that was when Little Eva came back after she was dead and she was a dream or a vision, like something in the Bible, that Uncle Tom had when he died.

That was how it was. Little Eva was really in a book, yet Little Eva was there on the stage and we saw her die, just like the book, Aunt Belle said, though we hadn't read it. Aunt Belle sat in the row back of us with Tootie and Tootie changed places with Gilbert (because he couldn't see very well) between the acts. Tootie liked Topsy best and Harold did too, I think.

Ida and Aunt Belle liked the song Little Eva's father sang when Little Eva's mother played the piano. We had to wait for them to finish that before we could see the blood-hounds. The bloodhounds did really chase Eliza on the ice. She screamed and jumped on the pieces of ice and you forgot that it wasn't ice at all. You forgot the people around you and that you were in the theater, you forgot you were in a town even, that you would have to go home after this. That is how it was. Everybody waited, and someone laughed when the bloodhounds sniffed round the lights in front of the stage and didn't chase Eliza. But I could see that they were not real terrible dogs. I could see that they were really very good dogs, yet at the same time, something else in me that listened when Ida reads us a fairy tale, would know that they were terrible and horrible dogs, that they would rush at Eliza and her baby, which was only a big bundled-up doll or even only a bundle, and tear at her and bite her to death. I mean, I would know that we were there, that Harold was beside me, and that Tootie had the place on the end that Harold had had, so that he could see down the aisle. Harold was next to me, where Gilbert had been.

There were three acts, they said. We had seen the first and second. There were small acts in between when they just dropped the curtain. In between the acts, everything was the same as when we came. There was red velvet on the seats of the chairs; a boy in a round cap went down the aisle sell-ing popcorn. Tootie said, "Could we have popcorn, Mama?" Aunt Belle bought us popcorn. But you could tell all the time, even when you were crackling your popcorn that everything was different. I mean, it went on even after the lights came up in the theater, even after people turned round in their seats and talked and the boys in the gallery shouted and stamped.

It was the university students in the gallery; Aunt Belle called them boys. They stamped and laughed and clapped and made a lot of whistling noises to the bloodhounds, when they came on the stage.

"Why do they laugh, Aunt Belle?"

"Oh—well—I mean, lots of them come from big cities or even from New York. I suppose they think it's just a funny little provincial theater."

"What's provincial, Aunt Belle?"

"Well, a small place, a little town, like ours; I mean to them, to lots of them, it's a funny old-fashioned show, that's why they laugh and have fun like they do, whistling at the wrong time to make the dogs forget to chase Eliza."

It was fun for the university boys to whistle and stamp their feet. But people hushed at them and a man in front turned round and said he'd speak to the manager about this, and in the last act when Uncle Tom died, maybe the man had spoken to the manager, because the university boys seemed to be quiet in the gallery.

The university boys were grown-up young men like our Howard cousins, and Eric and Alfred who were at the university, too. The thing was, it was very exciting and maybe the university boys thought it was exciting, too, but in a different sort of way. They did not understand how it is for some people. They did not understand that when Aunt Belle said would Gilbert mind coming back with her so Tootie could sit next to the aisle, that *aisle* all at once, was the same as the aisle in church. They could not understand how some people could sit like that in the chairs with the red velvet in the dark, and it was like being in church.

The theater was dark and the lights that Aunt Belle

called footlights were like ours in church, when we sit in rows, grown people and children like this, and the Sisters walk down the aisles to hand the candles to the children.

Lots of people do not know the things we know and that Uncle Tom was seeing a vision, like something in the Bible, when he saw Little Eva with a long nightdress and her gold hair, standing against the curtain that had wings painted on it, just where Little Eva was standing, so it made Little Eva look like the princess in our fairy book who had long gold hair, only the princess hadn't wings, only maybe the university boys didn't have that kind of book or maybe they didn't know how to look at pictures or to see things in themselves and then to see them as if they were a picture.

Anyhow it was over. We went home. But the street would never be the same again, it would always be different, really everything would always be different. This street that we walked along, deliberately dodging ahead to thwart Aunt Belle and Ida (who would prefer, we knew, the short way across the bridge and up the hill), was the street down which, only yesterday, Uncle Tom had been pulled, complete with log cabin; the hounds we had seen, less than an hour ago, chasing Eliza, had snuffled and shuffled their way along these very paving-stones. Here by the Linden House, the procession halted and the slaves pushed together and Simon Legree took off his hat and got out a cigar. I could have wished the parade had got stuck near the end, then I could have looked and looked at Little Eva, I could have pushed forward and touched a gold wheel of her chariot.

Here the donkeys had slowed down, and they had one donkey pulling a log, I suppose to show how the cabin was built. Well, really there had been so much, you kept remembering bits of it; in the light of the play itself, the details of the parade came into different perspective, everything came true—that is what it was. Everything came true.

The street came true in another world; our side street

past the Linden House in our small town that the university students, Aunt Belle said, would call provincial, was a street across which wheels of a great procession had passed. Oh well, I know it was only Little Eva in a jerry-built, gold chariot, and yet it was the very dawn of art, it was the sun, the drama, the theater, it was poetry—why, it was music, it was folklore and folksong, it was history. It was all these things, and in our small town, on the curb of the pavement, the three children—and maybe Tootie—who stood watching, were all the children of all the world; in Rome, in Athens, in Palestine, in Egypt they had watched golden chariots, they had seen black men chained together and cruel overseers brandishing whips. It was Alexandria, it was a Roman Triumph, it was a Medieval miracle-play procession with a devil, who was Simon Legree, and the poor dark shades of purgatory, who were the negroes chained together, and it was Pallas Athenè, in her chariot with the Winged Victory poised with the olive crown, who was coming to save us all.

It was all these things and many more, and the names of many cities could be woven together on a standard to be carried at the head of this procession, and yet you would not have told half the story. It was art or many of the arts, concentrated and maybe consecrated by the fixed gaze of these same American children, who in the intensity of their naive yet inherent or inherited perception, glorifying these shoddy strolling players, became one with their visionary mid-European ancestors and their Elizabethen English forebears.

And it didn't stop there, because when we got home everything was like that. If you take down one side of a wall, you have a stage. It would be like the doll house that had only three walls, and you could arrange the room without any trouble; a bed could be over there by the window instead of drawn up in the corner by the wall; Mama was sitting at the piano and it was still Mama and yet it was Little Eva's mother and if Uncle Fred came in and sang *Last night there were four Marys,* like he did when Mamalie asked him to, then he would be Little Eva's father.

Papa did not sing of course, and we would not want to change our father for anyone else and Uncle Fred was our uncle anyhow, but that is what you can do.

If Mama sits at the piano and plays *Moonlight,* the room is the same and there is always that difference that *Moonlight* makes when Mama plays it, but there was another difference. There would be someone else who was myself, yet who was the child of the Lady who Played the Piano; then I would be Little Eva and I would have an Uncle Tom who was not really an uncle, but it was like that. It was called a play, it was the first play we had been to. But a play and to play were the same, you could play now without any trouble. You could arrange the sofa that was too heavy to pull on the other side of the room and you could see how the room had only three sides and you could walk across the room and toss your head and say, "Oh, this is so hot, it's so heavy," and you could carefully push it aside when you sat down on a chair; although anyone could see that you had short hair with, at best, mousy duck-tails at the nape of the neck, yet you could toss your head and the gold curls.

It was the same gold as the princess had, who had the seven or the nine brothers, and I had brothers and could make up more by counting in the cousins. Then, I would be like that. But no one would know about it. Everything was the same, but everything was different. You could think about it in bed. Then everyone's house would be open on one side and you would see it all going on. The Williams family across the street would be in bed, at least most of them would be, but Olive maybe would be allowed to stay up and help Professor Williams put away the stones that he had in little boxes for his students at the university.

I did not want to think of the university and the students but of the Williams family across the street, and Papalie and Mamalie sitting in their sitting room, and Ida in the kitchen. I did not tell Gilbert about it, and I laughed when he laughed about how funny it was when the bloodhounds didn't chase Eliza but sniffed and scuffled in the footlights. The footlights threw new shadows, so that faces were different. Now I could see that their faces were different under the lamp in the dining room so that Mama said, "What's the matter, Sister? Why don't you eat your dinner?"

The dinner was on the table. The lamp was on the sideboard. The doors opened from the little hall that led into the kitchen and every time the door opened and Ida came in, you could see how the whole room was different. There was the door that led down steps to the street, that we called the side door; it was closed now. There was the door that led into the sitting room. Someone might come in, like they did, maybe Uncle Hartley with a newspaper or Aunt Jennie with a basket or even Mamalie with a plate and a napkin over it, "I know Charles likes my apple pies," she would say and Mama would take the plate and say, "Oh, Mimmie you do spoil us," and say, "Sit down Mimmie," and Mamalie would say, "But Francis" (that was Papalie) "is waiting for his dinner."

At any moment, someone might walk in the door through that street door or the closed sitting room door and you would see now how they said things, how Mama was sure to say, "Oh, Mimmie you spoil us," and Papa would look up and get up to find Mamalie a chair and then she would slide out; she is a very little lady; really, soon, Gilbert will be as tall as she is. You could see how pretty Mamalie was, in her lace cap.

Mama had been to a fortune-teller. I do not remember when she first told me about it, yet I remember the strange gap in consciousness, the sort of emptiness there, which I soon covered over with my childish philosophy or logic, when she said, "It's funny, the fortune-teller told me, I would have a child who was in some way especially gifted."

It was that, that stuck. We were not any of us "gifted," as if we had failed them somehow. I can not say why we cared, or maybe the others didn't care. But there should have been a child who was gifted. How could I know that this apparent disappointment that her children were not "gifted," was in itself her own sense of inadequacy and frustration, carried a step further?

Mama told me how she heard a voice outside one of the empty classroom doors.

"What voice, Mama?"

"Oh, it was only Papa, it was only Papa; he said, 'who is making this dreadful noise in here?' "

"Who was?"

"Well—I was alone, I went off, I was alone, I was hiding, I was singing."

"Oh—I see—didn't Papalie know?"

"Well—I don't know—I don't think he meant to hurt me, no, I know he didn't mean to hurt me."

"Maybe it was someone else making a noise in another classroom."

"No—maybe it was—yes, but anyhow, I was so hurt, I never sang any more, not even in church."

So Mama never sang any more, though her speaking voice had a rare quality; it was low and rich and vibrant. Yet, it couldn't have been just that that stopped Mama singing, there must have been other things as well. Anyhow, she told me that, and she told me how she went to a fortune-teller.

Mama did not tell me that the Spanish Student came

into the fortune-telling, but she did tell me about the Span-ish Student. I see the Spanish Student, in capital letters like that, like a play or an opera. It was perhaps a play or an opera to Mama, something that might have happened, which did not happen, in which she played a small part, in which she might have played a leading role.

She told me about Madame Rinaldo who had taught singing at the seminary, and who had been an opera singer, and the aunts often talked about her, and we still had some of the old things that Madame Rinaldo had left Mama—a crown, bracelets, stage properties, veils, and robes in an old chest in the attic. Madame Rinaldo did come into it, but Mama never said she imagined herself in Madame Rinaldo's crown and bracelets, though I often tried them on and wished I were enough grown-up so they would fit me, and like Mama, I pretended to sing when no one was around.

The Spanish Student was from South America; he was at the university.

Mama said, "There was a Spanish Student at the uni-versity—he—well, he thought that he was very fond of me. I was sorry afterwards." What was she sorry about? Was she sorry he had gone away or that she had not gone with him, or what?

"How do you mean you were sorry afterwards?"

"I mean," she said, "I forgot myself, I might almost have forgotten myself—I mean he was a stranger, he was a southerner, he did not understand—I mean, I never told Papa about it, I was sorry afterwards."

I waited for more.

She said, "He went away."

Madame Rinaldo died and left Mama her opera things, the Spanish Student went away, Mama met Papa at the semi-nary at German reading-classes they had for older people in the evenings. Mama said the fortune-teller was just like those people, she just happened to say this or to say that. I did wonder what she really did say. But Mama did tell me that the fortune-teller told her that she would have a child who was gifted.

"You know what these fortune-tellers are like," said Mama. "Of course we never told Papa."

☀ *THE DREAM*

The dog is now a myth, for that reason he appears in dreams, unmistakably and in the most satisfactory manner. He wallows in snowdrifts, his ears are like the knitted mittens on that long tape than ran through the sleeves of our winter coats; he carries, of course, the barrel strapped to his collar, and as I fling my arms about his neck—he is larger than a small pony—I am in an ecstasy of bliss. The snow gives back whatever an anesthetic may have once given.

Mythology is actuality, as we now know. The dog with his gold-brown wool, his great collar and the barrel, is of course none other than our old friend Ammon-Ra, whose avenue of horned sphinxes runs along the sand from the old landing-stage of the Nile barges to the wide portals of the temple at Karnak. He is Ammon or he is *Amen, forever and ever.* I want you to know he is as ordinary as the cheap lithograph that used to hang in nursery bedrooms; he is even as ordinary as the colored advertisement sheets, bearing his effigy, tacked to telegraph poles that one passed, in the old days, along the reaches of the *Bernese Oberland.* You see him on a postcard in a window along the lake of Lucerne. There is a monk standing beside him; we may whisper Saint Bernard. Or, depending on what particular line or telegraph pole our particular wire of approach to the eternal verities is strung, we may actually be reminded of our own or a friend's dog, or we may know that we have seen, in the flesh, the Lion of Saint Mark's or the Lion of Saint Jerome, or we may recognize our indisputable inheritance, Ammon, *Amen* from time immemorial, later Aries, our gold-fleece Ram.

Our Ram, however, had not gold fleece, his fleece came from Mamalie's medicine cupboard. It was pulled off in tufts from a roll of cotton for making bandages or for stuffing pillows or for putting in ears with a little oil or for borrowing to make a quilt for the new bed for the doll house. Cotton? Was this from a bush that grew in the South or was it from a sheep? I do not think we knew or asked; greater issues were at stake, greater questions though unasked were being answered.

It would be near Christmas again, because Papalie had a great lump of clay on his table, the microscope was put away on top of the bookcase, and the tray of pens for his red and green and black ink was pushed aside and he had just said, "Elizabeth," (which was Mamalie) "will you keep an eye on these ink bottles?" There was not a breath of suggestion that any of us might upset the ink bottles, there was nothing of that in his voice. He wanted room for the lump of clay that was wrapped in a damp cloth and the cotton wool and the roll of fine wire and the matchsticks.

You may wonder what mysterious occult ceremony requires cotton wool from Mamalie's medicine cupboard, a knot of wire and the gardening shears which did not belong on his desk, matchsticks, a lump of clay. You, yourself may wonder at the mystery in this house, the hush in this room; you may glance at the row of children on the horsehair sofa and at the plaque of mounted butterflies, or at the tiny alligator, who is varnished and looks like a large lizard and whose name is Castor or whose name is Pollux, the children can not tell you for no one has been able to answer that question for them.

Castor and Pollux are, you may know, stars shining in the heavens, but though two or three of the children seated on this sofa watch their father go out of the house on clear evenings to look at the stars in his little observatory across the bridge up the side of the mountain, this Castor and Pollux are not thus Greek, they are not stars in the sky, they are not even a myth out of a later, more grown-up fairy book called *Tanglewood Tales*.

They have not yet read the *Tanglewood Tales;* Ida reads Grimm to some of them at night after they are in bed, temporarily three in a row in the same bed.

Castor and Pollux are two alligators; one is dead, true to the Greek myth which after all came from the older Egyptian layer of thought and dream. Castor is, shall we say, hibernating in the attic in his tank behind the wire netting. Pollux, shall we say, is mounted on an oval of beautifully varnished wood, a talisman, a mascot, an image—an idol even. Men worshipped crocodiles in the days when men's minds were not more developed than the minds of this row of children.

Papalie is leading them out of Egypt but they do not know that. He is leading them to the Promised Land which is just around the corner, only a week or a few days, for this is part of Christmas. You may wonder what a lump of clay and matchsticks has to do with Christmas, but if you are a stranger in our town, you will be told, if you will wait quietly in the other room under the picture of Jedediah Weiss who is Mamalie's father, who is dead. If you belong to the town, you will know all about Christmas, I mean the real Christmas with a *putz* under the tree. If you are a stranger, you will say, "What a funny word, I mean, I don't understand," and Mamalie will say, "Oh, it's German but we never found another word for it." If you are well-informed, you may say, "I suppose it derives from something." *"Putzen,"* Mamalie may say, "to decorate or to trim."

It is part of the tree, the most important part, the children think. "It is what you put," says Tootie, "I think; I think *putz* is what you *put* on the moss," and they all laugh, for Tootie is very quick and clever, they say, not like the Professor's children who are so quiet, but the Professor's children do talk sometimes. Gilbert the oldest, who is two years older than Hilda, talks quite a lot and makes jokes. Once walking on the mountains with Papalie, he saw an old goat that belonged to some of the shanty-people, as they called them, behind the mills. "Look, Papalie," he said, "look at that goat, it looks like you, Papalie."

Everybody told that story often; Gilbert was rather bored with it. He had said it when he was only a little boy, younger than Tootie even, who now said things they thought were quick and clever and cute. Papalie came back and told them the story. Hilda, who is the only girl, sitting between Gilbert and Tootie, wondered a long time about it. "Does he look like a goat, Mamalie?" Mamalie laughed and said, "It was just his white beard and maybe the way his hair curled over his ears." Papalie's hair is not like goats' horns, but if you look and look at him, maybe he is like a goat. Hilda never thought it was so funny, though they always laughed and kept on telling it, though now Tootie said the funny things, like *"Putz* is a place where you *put* things under the Christmas tree."

What he did was, he took his ivory paper-knife and cut off an edge of the lump of clay. The clay lay on the damp cloth, like the dough Ida mixed in our kitchen. He turned back the edges of the cloth around the clay. He took the clay in his hands and rolled it, like Ida makes a biscuit. He pulled at one end, and you knew exactly that it would not look like a sheep. But when he jabbed two points in the face and drew a line for a mouth with the handle of his pen, you knew exactly what it was; it was eyes and a sheep-mouth, though it would not show very much until he had finished several sheep and put them aside to dry.

Afterwards, he would ink in the eyes with black ink and draw a little line in red ink for the mouth. What he did was, he made several sheep like that in a row, like Ida's biscuits on the kitchen table.

He pulled the cotton wool into little puffs and stuck the puffs of wool on the sheep. But first he stood them up on legs, that is what the matchsticks were for, and the burnt-out ends of the matchsticks were the sheep's hooves. He made small sheep too, those were the lambs, and at the end, he made one large sheep. This was the special moment. He cut off bits of wire from the small coil of wire, he bent the wire into shape, he stuck in the wire horns. All this time, we were sitting on the sofa. The sheep stood up on their matchstick legs, but he would not put in their faces until they were quite dry.

He also had little pointed bits of stiff paper which he had inked red for their ears. That is what he did. Later, before we went to bed, when we were a bit older, say, two years older, Mama would get down the old boxes of Christmas-tree things from the attic and open them on the dining room table. From inside the crinkled faded tissue paper that a glass ball was wrapped in, there would come a sort of whisper, and a sprinkling of tiny old dead pine needles would fall on the table, from last year's tree.

We carefully unwrapped the balls, not remembering, hardly remembering anything of what had happened last Christmas but how under the carpet, it would be impossible, even if you wanted to, to shut out the "thing" that the fallen pine needles on the table conjured up; there was the moment when it began to happen, when indeed it had happened; that was not the exact moment when the boxes were set down on the table, not even the moment that Mama unknotted the old bit of red ribbon fastened round the flat somewhat-battered cardboard box that had cardboard compartments for the separate glass balls. The compartments were not full, for some glass balls were always broken, but we would go to the five-and-ten and get some more balls, some more silver or gilt lengths of trimming, as we called it, though it was all trimming.

On the table, we made separate heaps of the things; the glass balls in their open box were gone over, like toys in a toy-hospital. It was this special moment when Mama said, "See if you can find the end of an old candle, Sister, among the paper cornucopias," that the "thing" began.

The "thing" could not begin if there were not an old end or several almost burnt-out stumps of last year's beeswax candles. Whoever untrimmed the tree never forgot those candle-ends. It had to be the beeswax candles, the special candles that were used for the children's Christmas Eve service; the red and pink and blue and green five-and-ten boxes of candles could be seen all the year round, at home or anywhere, on anybody's birthday cake.

But this was another sort of birthday; it was, of course, exactly, the birthday of the Child in the manger, in whose honor we had arranged the sheep on the moss, yet it was something else, indefinable yet deeply personal, something our perception recognized though our thought did not then relate our Child to the other Holy Children, His racial or spiritual or mythological predecessors. We arranged the sheep on the moss, but we did not think of Amen-Ra or the Golden Fleece, or even Abraham and Isaac. We gathered the moss ourselves, on trips to the mountains, or Uncle Hartley or Uncle Bob would make an excuse to get the moss for us. "Helen, all the thick moss has been pulled off the rocks for miles around, it's too far for the children." If it were a snowy December, the aunts and uncles might hire a sleigh and go off together and come back, screaming and laughing, with bunches of mountain laurel. *Fir trees and pine and the laurel bough, We are twining in wreathes to greet thee now.*

It was not only a small Child in a manger, in a stable, in a town that had the same name as our town. It was not only those wooden Wise Men that Aunt Millie had on their *putz* or the star that was clipped onto the highest single up-standing top-spray of the tree. It was not only the smell of the moss, it was not only the smell of the spiced ginger-dough that was waiting under a cloth in the biggest yellow bowl on the pantry shelf, and yet it was all these; it was all these and the forms of the Christmas cakes, the lion, the bear, the lady with no arms, like Mrs. Noah, the oak leaf, the round circle we called the moon, the actual star, the other animals.

The "thing" was that we were creating. We were "making" a field under the tree for the sheep. We were "making" a forest for the elk, out of small sprays of a broken pine-branch. We ourselves were "making" the Christmas cakes. As we pressed the tin mold of the lion or the lady into the soft dough, we were like God in the first picture in the Doré Bible who, out of chaos, created Leo or Virgo to shine for-ever in the heavens. "We" were like that, though we did not know it. Our perception recognized it, though our minds did not define it. God had made a Child, and we children in return now made God; we created Him as He had created us, we created Him as children will, out of odds and ends; like magpies, we built Him a nest of stray bits of silver thread, shredded blue or rose or yellow colored paper; we knew our power. We knew that God could not resist the fragrance of a burning beeswax candle!

There was the prickly sting of the pine needles under the rope that fastened the branches. The tree was standing on the back porch, looped round so that it stood up thin and stiff; at this moment, a child's very ribs and diaphragm would be changed for a whole year with that deep intake of breath as Ida or Mama or even the new gardener cut the thick cord that bound the limbs; living limbs were bound and cramped in their rope cage.

There was that actual intake of breath (and the almost unbearable outbreathing of joy bordering on ecstasy) when the cord fell on the floor and nobody cared, nobody stopped to pick it up, though after Ida might call through the swing doors from the dining room, "Will one of you children undo these knots for me—this is good twine—and put it in the kitchen drawer."

No; we will not undo her knots for her. We have other things to do, we are busy. Mama has bought a new pot of paste, "Unscrew the top, Gilbert, will you. There is a brush, too, where have I put it? Harold, run out to the kitchen and fill a glass with water. Where are my scissors? What a lot of old needles this year—take care—here, spill them out on this," and she spreads out a piece of brown wrapping paper, "we'll put all the scraps on this. That tinsel looks pretty dull, but perhaps we can use it once more at the back of the tree, for filling in. Maybe, you'll find the top of this ball among the papers, Sister, if not, you can fasten a lump of wax to stick the hook in, you know how to do it. Here—" she finds the little candlestump.

There is still a frayed edge of the original red paper around the base, stuck to the wax. "I wonder whose candle this was, did you have a green or a red one last year?" Hilda cannot remember. Last year is a very, very long way off. Last year just after Christmas, they moved from the old town and the old house to this new big house that was built with the new transit house and the new observatory that wasn't yet finished, for Papa, when they asked him to come to the university in Philadelphia. Philadelphia, even, is quite a long way off, Papa goes in to teach his students at the classes there. Papa is out now at his transit house; he may come in at any moment in his high boots and his fur cap, like a Russian in that picture they had at the Widows' House that Mama said she and Aunt Laura made up stories about.

*Zeisberger** preaching to the Indians* is hanging in the sitting room, *Washington at Mount Vernon* is in the hall; the same clock is ticking in the hall that Mamalie's papa himself made. It is a grandfather's clock, it was made by Mama's grandfather.

Everything is the same, yet in the great tide-wave of moving everything is different. What fun to move; "Papa is going to a bigger university, they are building him a transit house." "What's a transit house?" "I don't know, it's something important." They felt alienated but important before they left, and the last Christmas tree was not quite like the others, but the reason for that—Papalie was dead, there was a new baby.

There was the painful wrench from the school but that pain too was mitigated; Miss Helen was leaving to get married, anyway. She gave each of her children a *carte-de-visite* photograph as Aunt Jennie called them; the reason, Aunt Jennie said, was that the photograph was not much larger than a visiting card. There were visiting cards from the Philadelphia ladies who came to call. There were many visiting cards on the Dresden platter on the table in the hall.

Rosa Bonheur's *Horse Fair* was set on an easel in the front room. There were two rooms with big folding doors; there had been two rooms with folding doors in the old

* A Moravian missionary

house. We folded the doors and pinned up a sheet for the magic lantern or for pinning on the donkey's tail. There had been parties like that with the children up and down the street; now the children, the nearest, were two miles away. The school was a public school; "The children are too young," Mama would explain to the university ladies, "to send in to town yet." The new school was horrible.

There was something horrible about the school. We took lunch in a basket and did not get back until four. At the old school we went home at noon for lunch and did not go back to school until two, and then home at four. There were hours which were torture, it was too far to walk home in that noon hour and back. There was twelve to one for lunch. Now time included a new factor, a school clock in a public school ticked differently from the church clock in the old town. There was no doubt about it. There was nothing to do because Gilbert didn't seem to mind and ran off and played baseball with the other older boys, but Harold was lonely with no child to play with.

Hilda felt Harold's pain and loneliness but could not translate it into words. Later, she learned to get through the hour by skipping rope with the other girls, children from the near farms and from the small village. "It's not that they're *common*." There were no words for it. They were different, they were younger in mind and reasoning; "Don't think I will make any distinction with your children," one of the teachers had said to Mama. It was a funny way for anyone to talk to Mama. We go to a public school; that is not what is wrong. It isn't that the room *smells* differently, it's the way the clock ticks on the wall.

Now there were sounds. There was the crinkling of the paper as Mama swept aside the pieces from the old box;

there had been the rustle of the old pine needles, yet it was very quiet. Ida was opening the stove lid, she was pouring in coal from the coal scuttle. She would lock the back door. It was dark outside. There was a big maple tree in front of the house; they had built the house just there because of the three big maple trees. There were no other trees. The ground had been ploughed up, it had been an old cornfield. There would be a lawn, they would put up the sundial that was now in the empty room in the wing that was to have the university books later.

The wing was empty. There were three rooms upstairs in the wing and an extra bathroom, and downstairs, the big empty library and the hall with the wing door, as we called it. Papa was expecting an assistant to live there, and maybe Eric would come too. Eric and Mr. Evans, whom we had just met, would move into the wing later; then the wing would be full. Now the wing was empty. Ida had a big room over the kitchen. There was Annie, too, but Annie was sitting upstairs with the baby.

There was a farm beyond, fields, and cows in a shed. The wind blew through the maple branches, and Ida had put down the coal scuttle. Harold had brought back the glass of water for the paste brush. "Here, give it to me, Gilbert," Mama said, for Gilbert had not been able to unscrew the top of the new paste pot. In a minute, maybe Papa would come in with his beard and his fur cap and his high boots, then maybe Mama would send us all to bed. This minute must last forever. It would last forever.

The clock in the hall ticked off this minute, so this minute belonged to the clock in the hall, it belonged to Mamalie and to Papalie who was dead. The clock in the hall would strike but even if it struck, it would not matter. Now Mama did not send us off to bed so early. Mama was unscrewing the top of the new paste pot. She set it down on the table and put the sticky lid on the brown paper. All around us were the table, the dining room chairs, the sideboard and the china cupboard with dishes that Aunt Mary (who wasn't a real aunt) had painted for Mama's wedding, with bluebells and daisies and wild roses.

The university ladies would say, "But aren't you afraid, cut off like this, miles from a doctor?" Then they would hush their voices and whisper behind the folding door, you could almost hear what they said. The folding door might be shut but even so, there was a large crack; "Now run along Hilda" or "Run along Sister," Mama would say, and I would go out, maybe possibly to ask Ida to bring in tea on a tray. It was different here, the ladies had to hear everything over and over, maybe even, one had not heard of the Moravians or the Bach choir, or else like Mrs. Schelling, they would talk about Vienna and where they had gone.

Mama had been to Europe on her honeymoon; there were the pictures. *Paul Potter's Bull* was over the bench in the hall that had a lid and was a box really for our leggings and our overshoes. The *Venus de Milo* was in the sitting room, there were those two rooms and now here, the dining room. There was a narrow hall with two swing doors from the dining room to the kitchen. There was a hen on the chest across the table. It showed just over Harold's head. It was a white hen. It was sitting on a china basket; if you picked it up, you saw that it was hollow, the china nest was for boiled eggs. Mamalie had one too, hers was grey and speckled. The hen sat on the dresser opposite the table. It was the same hen that had sat on the same dresser in the old dining room.

Aunt Jennie brought Hilda some Chinese lily bulbs and showed her how to plant them in a bowl with water and pebbles. Mama said Hilda could have them in their bowl in the old dining room on the window ledge. There was that window that looked out on the alley, which was really not an alley but a lane, but Uncle Hartley said *allée* was French really, and maybe their alley was named *allée* by the Marquis de Chastellux when he came to visit the town. Uncle Hartley made fun of all the old things, and all the same they were true, Aunt Aggie said.

There were two other windows in the old dining room and a door, through a hall like this, to the kitchen, and another door leading up a few steps to the back stairs and through to the kitchen that way. There were two other windows in the old dining room, but rather dark as they opened on the porch that was roofed over and anyhow, had the vines growing.

This room has four windows, set even, like windows in a doll house. The table is in the middle. There are three doors; one leads out to the hall, one to the sitting room, one to the kitchen. Hilda seemed to be running this over ritualistically in her head, as if it were necessary to remember the shape of the house, each room, the hen on the dresser, the dishes shut away in the sideboard, before she dared turn her eyes actually to the table, to the tangled heap of tarnished tinsel, to the empty box that had held the glass balls, to the miscellaneous collection of gilt stars, red, blue and pink cornucopias and paper chains that were torn, that Mama called the paper things; there were dolls too in that lot, several babies in paper gilt highchairs, some dancers in fluffed-out short white petticoats, standing on one toe, and angels sprinkled with glistening snow that was beginning to peel off.

Ida said could she go upstairs, was there anything, but she stood at the door. She had on her blue kitchen-apron. She came in and the door swung-to behind her. She looked at the things on the table. She said, "Could I take the baby in my room?" She wanted the baby in her room. I should have liked the baby in my room, but he did not like me very much. Mama said, "Leave him in the crib if he is asleep." Ida might wake him up, she could, why couldn't she take him to her room? What did the Philadelphia ladies whisper about? The house was very quiet. The clock in the hall ticked—you could hear it tick even if you did not stop to listen. There was scraping on the front doorsteps, that might be Papa coming in—or it might be—what did the Philadelphia ladies think could happen?

We were not all alone, there was Mama, there was Ida, there was Annie with the baby upstairs. Upstairs seemed rather far away. In the old house, the clock was at the top of the stairs, and the stairs went straight up; here they turned on a landing and you could not slide down the bannisters. On the stair wall were some of the photographs of Venice; there was a lady too, lying on the ground with a big book open and a skull (like Papa's Indian skull on his bookcase); she was someone in the Bible, Mary-someone in a cave with long hair.

We would get some small rocks from the stream that ran in the little valley several fields below the house, for the cave on the *putz*. Ida had found another box on the floor; she said, "You've forgotten a box on the floor." Gilbert said, "No, I put it there." Ida lifted the box from the floor, none of us had forgotten it, it was a heavy cardboard box tied with string. It was the most important. It was the box with the animals and the little hut and the wooden fence that folded up, that would run round the edge of the moss and make a field for the sheep to graze in. Ida said, "Where are the scissors?" She cut the string of the box.

There was a picture of Pandora and her box in the *Tanglewood Tales* that Miss Helen read us, Friday afternoons if we were good, instead of lessons. Pandora let all evil things out of the box, but there was one good thing left; Miss Helen explained it was a myth. The good thing left was hope.

Everything would turn evil in the box but there was hope left, after everything evil had flown out.

We knew what was in this box, it was an ordinary cardboard box, a large one of very tough brown paper. Ida started to roll up the string the way she did, then came to the knots and looked at the string. Then she dropped it on the spread-out brown paper that was for the scraps. It was not time to take out the animals, we did the Christmas-tree things first, but now Gilbert jerked at the top of the box that did not fit like a lid, but was like a box over another box. It stuck and Gilbert jerked at it.

Ida said to Gilbert, "Hold the box." She got her fingers under the edges and worked the top of the box up; it stood like a box on a box, and Gilbert's head above it was like the jack-in-the-box when the little wire catch is pushed off the fastener of a jack-in-the-box box.

Jack and Jill went up the hill. *Gil Blas* was the name of a book Uncle Hartley had, but Gil was a man and not Jack. "I mean, if I am Jill in the picture, the way we played when we were children," thought Hilda, "then I would be Gil who is short for Gilbert, but we never call him Gil but Gib sometimes." He did everything first, he made up games for things when we were children, he called me Deetie, people call me Deetie sometimes, that was Gilbert's name for Sister Mama would explain and people would laugh. Sister or Deetie or other names, but if I were Jill, I would be Gil, we would be "twins." There were the two alligators at Papalie's who were twins; they were called Castor and Pollux.

Castor and Pollux, Eric had told us, were really stars in the sky. Ida said, "Take care, don't jerk at it" and pushed Gilbert's hands away. Harold slid down the chair and stood looking. Mama called, "Is that you Charles?" as the front door opened and then shut and Papa came across the hall in his boots; he said *"Töcterlein,"* not looking at Mama. Papa is not a Moravian, he does not go to church, he met Mama at a German class at the old seminary when Papalie was principal there. I got up and took Papa's hand. It is me he calls *Töcterlein,* though that is a German word and Papa is not German. They were not all German really, Mama would explain to the university ladies, they came from Moravia and Bohemia and England, though they had Germans too and Danes in the brotherhood that came to America from *Herrnhut,* where they went from Moravia when Count Zinzendorf helped them to get to America.

Some of the very old ladies in the old town could not talk English very well, and Papalie had some German books, but Papa had German books, too, about the stars. Gilbert interrupted, jerking at the box lid, and now maybe Mama won't cut out the gilt paper for new stars. We paste the gilt paper on cut-out cardboard, both sides, and hang the stars on the tree with a bent bit of wire or with gilt thread threaded through a darning needle.

The needles are on the table, the whole of Mama's workbasket is on the table. There is a strawberry of wax for thread and a strawberry with emery powder for sharpening needles and getting the rust off. There are all these things on the table and Ida is still here and it will get late. The clock will strike. Papa will want his late-evening supper, maybe he wants it now. "I'm going out again," said Papa, as if he knew what I was thinking, but he looked round the table, as if he came from another world, another country; he was a Russian, his fur cap was in his other hand, he was a pathfinder, he had worked on the northern boundary before he came to Lehigh University at Bethlehem.

What it was, was Mama had Uncle Fred and Uncle Hartley and Aunt Laura and Aunt Aggie and Mamalie and the old school and Cousin Ed and everybody in the old town really. She had Gilbert and the new baby upstairs. She had Harold.

Ida and Annie belonged to the house and the kitchen and the baby.

What Papa had was the transit house now and his classes at the university and people who came to see him about the new instruments and reporters from the papers. What Papa had was outside, the old observatory on the hill, the walk across the bridge at night, "like a thief or an astronomer," as he would say. What he had was the high walled-in bookshelves here and in the old study, the same but with strips of trimmed leather with brass-headed tacks along each shelf. There was the smell of leather; his old gloves had the fingers cut off so that he could manage all those little screws that were so important on his instruments.

He had a broom in the corner of his transit house which was really a little house with windows and shutters that opened the whole roof. Snow blew in and he kept a broom to sweep out the snow from inside his house. What he was, was a pathfinder, an explorer. It was cold outside. He went out in the middle of the night again; he would lie down on his sofa in his study or he would sleep in the afternoon. He was outside this, he was outside everything, where was he? If he came in, everything was different, he was cold, his hand was cold. His fingers were long. My hand was small in his hand. "You have hands like your father," they said. He said his one girl was worth all his five boys put together. He should not say that. It made a terrible responsibility, it made one five times as much as one should be.

They said, "She is quiet like her father." They said, "It's funny the children aren't gifted with such a brilliant father."

What was this gift? It took him out of doors, sometimes several different times at night after we were all in bed. He had a lantern like a captain on a ship. He had thermometers, he had glass prisms in his new transit house that Mr. Evans was coming to work with; they made different rainbows of different stars. Mr. Evans told us that, the one time he came. He said he wanted to work with the new instruments because stars were suns, didn't we know that?

What would happen now? He was not this, he was kind about it, was he really interested?

He had never had a Christmas tree when he was a child.

There was Alvin, who was killed or who died of typhoid fever in the Civil War, there was Papa, there was Aunt Rosa, there was Mercy. Mercy had died when she was a very little girl. I held on to Papa's hand. What it was, was there was Mercy, he told me Mercy had done a sampler, Mercy had read the Bible through before she was five—was that possible? Mercy had asked to give the kitten that was going to be drowned a saucer of milk, before it was drowned. That was all, absolutely all, that I ever knew about Mercy.

He said, "Mercy," and gave a little neighing laugh like a horse, "fed the kitten a saucer of milk before it was drowned."

Where was the sampler? Had Aunt Rosa the sampler? Aunt Rosa was very quiet, she and Uncle John had been missionaries. She watched us trim the tree one Christmas and did not seem to understand; that is, she did not help us, as if she did not know how to trim a Christmas tree.

No one seemed to belong to Papa when he came in out of the cold, though Mama looked up and Ida said, "Will the Professor want his evening supper now or later?" Everything revolved around him; Mama was sweeping up the bits of gilt paper, she seemed to be thinking of something else. Harold stood looking, Gilbert did not shout now. It was as if he brought into the house the night and the cold, and when he laughed, it was not like Uncle Fred or Uncle Hartley, it was a sort of snort like a horse makes. "Does the Professor's beard really freeze on his instrument?" the university ladies would ask. Sometimes, they seemed to think it very funny, sometimes they were serious and said, "Such devotion" or something of that sort.

Yes it was true, he must be cold out there alone with the snow drifting into the transit house. Who understood this? Who understood what he was doing? Mama didn't. "I can't follow my husband's work," she would say to the ladies, "I don't pretend to."

Papa did not tell us what he was doing. Mr. Evans seemed very surprised that we did not know all about it. "Your father is doing very important work," he said. "I suppose he's explained it to you, on variation of latitude." We did not dare ask Mr. Evans what that was. Some day, I would ask Papa. I did not want to know really. What it was, was that he was separate, he was not really part of this table with the glass balls, with the tinsel paper, with the workbasket, with the paste pot, with the old gilt fir cones that Mama said we could paint over with some new gilt that she would get when she went in to shop in Philadelphia.

But once at Christmastime, he had taken us out, as if what he did must be different.

He said, "I want to take the children out."

Mama said, "But now? It's late, it's snowing."

He said, yes he wanted to take the children; we were surprised. Mama and Ida got our coats and mittens, there was snow on the ground and the lamps were lit along Church Street; we walked along with Papa in the snow, in the dark, after dinner along Church Street.

The snow swirled around the lampposts and ahead, you could see the circle like an island where the next lamp was. We got past the grocer's and on down the empty street; we turned at the end by the seminary, up Main Street where the stores were. We stopped in front of the big toystore or the big store that had all the toys in the window for Christmas, and he told us to stand there and look at the toys and find out what we wanted.

We did not know what to ask for, for day after tomorrow or tomorrow was Christmas. We went in and he said, could we find something that we would all like, something that we could all have together. That seemed hard at first, but it was very easy really for we found a box of animals; then the lady in the store found a bigger box; there were animals set in cardboard, there were about twelve large animals.

The lady said they were from abroad.

There was a polar bear, a camel, an elephant, each an animal in itself, not like the Noah's Ark animals.

We brought the box home. Mama said, "But it's not Christmas." Papa said he got us our present now; "But they better keep it," said Mama. But we said we knew what was inside. Gilbert held the box, he would not let Ida take it, we took it upstairs, we could have it upstairs if we would go to bed, "It is very late," said Mama.

Papa shook out the snow from his hat and put his cane in the hat rack. Ida said, "That was quite a treat going out after dark, wasn't it?" We said, "Yes."

Those animals were still in the box, and they had lasted, they had not broken, they were very good animals, a little larger than the usual animals, but not too large for the *putz*. How often had they stood on the *putz* under the branches, was it two times or was it three times?

We had divided them up, each taking one, then coming round again and each choosing one. Gilbert had first choice and took the elephant, but I did not care; for first, I wanted the deer with antlers, and Harold afterwards said, for first, he wanted the polar bear, so we each got our first animal; this was the way we divided things.

We had done this with the Punch and Judy show; of course naturally Gilbert had Punch and I had Judy and then Harold chose Joey, the clown, and he said he liked Joey better. In a way, I liked Joey better too, but it was natural for Gilbert to have Punch, me Judy, like Jack and Jill went up the hill.

Now there were these other animals, one had almost forgotten them, not quite; that was part of it; it was necessary almost-to-forget between the seasons, then the things came almost-as-a-surprise. There were those animals. Mama had given away the Punch and Judy show when we moved and some of our books. She had not given away the Christmas-tree things, they were still here, or weren't they? Suppose we opened the box and found that the polar bear was gone or the deer with antlers? Must Papa wait? Yet it was Papa who took us out, everything was different, we had never been out in the snow at night. The snow whirled round the lampposts and each lamppost was an island with its circle of light on the snow.

Even the snow was different, it looked different, it smelled different. It swirled round the lamps and the circle under the lamps. We had crossed the road that runs across Church Street to the bridge and the way along the river to the boats, but we never went there in the winter, nor to the island where he took us on Sundays in the summer because he was very unhappy when he was a little boy on Sunday. That is what I knew about him; he was not happy on Sunday and he had not had a Christmas tree.

He went out in the dark, but that night it was snowing so he did not go to his observatory across the river but took us out. The snow blew round the lamps, and we had crossed the street that runs downhill to the bridge, we had passed Papalie's house which was really next door to us. Uncle Hartley and Aunt Belle lived there too, and we were going down Church Street, past the Bell House and the Sisters' House and the Widows' House and the old seminary and the church where we had our Christmas-Eve candles.

This must have been on the day before Christmas Eve or was it Christmas Eve?

It was a day set apart; for the first time, we went out in the dark in the snow. Harold was small and had to be pulled a little, but Papa did not carry him. Gilbert ran ahead to the lamppost ahead and then turned round and waited for us. He scraped up some snow for a snowball and looked round, but there were none of the schoolboys to throw it at.

There was no one on the street, there were no marks of wheels or footsteps across the street.

There were lights in the Sisters' House windows. The clock struck but I forgot to count it. It was the church clock. We turned round below the walls of the church that was built up, with steps going up. Then we were on Main Street and there were people in the snow, even with umbrellas and carrying packages. He stopped in front of the window where the toys were.

Papalie was dead. There would be some of the clay sheep he made for us, new each year, or maybe there wouldn't be. The wool pulled off and got dirty but maybe Mama saved the last clay sheep; they would be the last, with the ram with the wire horns and the lambs with matchstick legs and one or two lambs lying down without legs.

That was the thing.

That was why I waited and why I wondered if maybe Mama had given away the animals, it would be terrible; it had been so terrible that I forgot to care, I did not really care after the first minute, when we came to the new house and everything was empty, with no curtains, and we slept on mattresses on the floor.

In the empty room, the next day, I said, when Ida and Mama were unpacking the wooden boxes, "Can I have my Grimm?"

Mama looked at Ida and Ida looked in the box where the books were, "I can't find it," said Ida, "there is so much to do, run along, run along, ask the packing-man where he put the hammer."

Mama looked at Ida, there was something wrong.

"But I'll look," I said; then Mama said, "Oh, I remember now" and Ida went out herself to find the hammer.

"I thought at the last, as the fairy book was all coming to pieces"—I knew the worst.

In the new house, with everything empty and no clock ticking in the hall, I knew that something dreadful was going to be told. It was so dreadful that I really didn't care. Didn't Mama say we were getting so old now, didn't she add

"Some poor child who could not have a book," didn't she say—what did she say? It was the first thing I asked for when they began unpacking the boxes, but it did not matter. How could it? It was only an old book, it was falling to pieces, she had given it away, some other child. I forgot it then, or rather . . . the pictures came true in my head.

I could see the first picture, the bright princess with the ball and the frog in the corner to the left and then the large dancing bear and the girl going up the glass mountain with spikes she stuck in the ice sides of the mountain.

I was part of the ice of the mountain, it had happened long ago.

I did not care. Why should I? There was the princess with the brothers, she had long hair and lilies in her arms, there were ravens and the little hut in the forest. All that had been given away. It was not possible—you cannot give away yourself with a star on your forehead and your brothers flying over a tower above a forest and a hut in the woods.

That was the book, it had gone anyway now; Grimm was the children's Bible, Mama used to say. It was fairy tales, but so was the Greek myth *Tanglewood Tales* that Miss Helen read in school. It was the same kind of thing, it was real. It went on happening, it did not stop.

It was like the old man on Church Street. He was on the other side of Church Street across the alley; the alley was really a lane with bushes; the bushes ran up one side to the street where Miss Macmullen who had the kindergarten lived, past the Williams' house. It was the Williamses who said that Papalie was our grandfather.

I was running along the other side of the street with Gilbert and some of the cousins and some of the boys that Gilbert played with. We all stood outside the iron rails where the old man lived. He was with his gardener, the young man who had a knife or a pair of garden scissors in his belt. The old man looked at us. The garden was narrow with a path between the wall of the next house and his own house.

He was a tall old man with a white beard. He said, "Let the girl in." I was the only girl in the crowd of Gilbert and the cousins and the other boys. So I stood at the gate and looked at the path and felt strange, but I was the only girl so I stepped across the gate-stone to the path in the garden.

The old man said, "What do you want, you can have whatever you want from my garden." I looked around and I saw a tall lily plant; I said, "I want a lily," so the gardener or whoever he was, the young man took a knife from his belt or his pocket and cut off a white lily.

Then I went back, but the boys had all gone, Church Street was empty. I went in our front door and Mamalie and Mama were sitting in our sitting room like they did, talking and sewing. I showed them the lily, it was just the lily with hardly any stem; they said, "But it would be lovely on Papalie's grave," so I stuck it in the earth that was not yet grown over with grass, on Papalie's grave.

Then the old man said he would send his sleigh whenever the girl wanted it, so the gardener who was the coachman, came with the sleigh. The streets were all empty, but we drove round the town. I sat with my back to the driver and Mama sat with one boy on either side, under the fur rugs. "Whenever you want the sleigh, just ask me," said the old man. "It is because the girl asks; if she asks, I will send the sleigh."

One day I said to Mama, "What has become of the old man on Church Street who sent me a sleigh?" Mama said there was no old man on Church Street who sent us a sleigh. I said, "But don't you remember, I sat with my back to the driver who was the young man who cut off the lily for me that you and Mamalie told me to put on Papalie's grave, that I did put on Papalie's grave." Mama said no, she didn't tell me anything like that. Anyhow . . . when I came to think about it, this was the odd thing; the lily was flowering and the streets were full of snow. It could not be worked out. But it happened. I had the lily, in my hand.

Now Papa's hand was in my hand.

He called me *Töcterlein* and I couldn't help it. It made a deep cave, it made a long tunnel inside me with things rushing through.

There was another book with a picture; Mama cut it out. Because Mama cut it out, it was there always. People do not cut out pictures from their books; sometimes the pictures work loose, but they can be pasted back with that sort of paper that Uncle Hartley showed us that Papalie had for his special plates that had to be put in the book when he was making up the book he wrote about water-things that grow in water, that he showed us under the microscope. You could see what Papalie showed you. You could not see what it was that Papa went out to look at.

The picture was a girl lying on her back, she was asleep, she might be dead but no, Ida said she was asleep. She had a white dress on like the dress the baby wore in the photograph Aunt Rosa sent Mama, that Mama tried to hide from us, of Aunt Rosa's baby in a long white dress in a box, lying on a pillow. The baby looked as if it were asleep, the girl in the picture looked as if she were dead, but the baby was dead and the girl was asleep and the picture was called *Nightmare*.

The book was about *Simple Science,* someone gave it to us when we could not read, but Ida told us what the pictures were about. We knew about the snow anyway, we knew the snow was stars, that each snowflake had a different shape; we knew that and we knew about the kettle, at least we had seen the kettle in the kitchen with steam coming out. It seemed a funny thing to put in the book, but it was, Ida said, to explain how the steam happened, but I did not care about that. What I wanted to know was, what was a nightmare, was the nightmare real?

It was like an old witch on a broomstick, it was a horrible old woman with her hair streaming out and she was riding on a stick, it was a witch on a broomstick, but the book was science, they said it was to explain real things. Then a witch was real; in Grimm it was a fairy tale but a witch in a book called *Simple Science* that someone gave us must be real because Ida said that was what science was. Papa and Papalie were working at real things, called science; the old witch was riding straight at the girl who was asleep. It was a dream; Ida said, "Nightmare is a dream. That picture is to explain what a nightmare is."

We did not like that book, we did not notice when it was lost or given away. It was only the one picture. Mama said one of the children had screamed in the night that a nightmare was coming. It must have been Harold, for I do not remember that I screamed. But somebody screamed, it could not have been Gilbert, Harold said it was not him.

It was only a picture, I cut it out," she said; you could see how she had cut it, the picture was gone.

"What is a nightmare?"

"It's a name for a bad dream."

"Why is it a mare? Uncle Hartley said a mare is a mother horse."

"I don't know."

"Is it a night horse?"

"Well, no, I don't know, it's only a dream anyhow."

A nightmare is a mare in the night, it is a dream, it is

something terrible with hooves rushing out to trample you to death. It is death. It is the child with the ruffles on her nightgown who they say is asleep, but she is dead. Or is it Aunt Rosa's baby who they said is dead, but maybe it is asleep?

He goes out in the night.

"What does he do there? Why does he go across the bridge to his observatory?"

"I've told you and told you and *told* you, he goes out to look at the stars."

"Why?"

"Because that is his work, it is his—work—well he is a professor, isn't he? They give him money for teaching students, if he did not make money, where would you be, you wouldn't have a house, you would have no clothes to wear."

That is what he does. He goes out to look at the stars. Of course, now we are so much older, it is very simple; anyhow his transit house is here just across the field that will be a lawn next spring and they will put up the sundial that says *Tempus Fugit* which Mama says is time flies. Time flies. He goes out to look at stars that have something to do with time flying, Mr. Evans said, that has something to do with winter and summer and the way the earth goes round the sun. "The earth goes round the sun," said Mr. Evans. As if we didn't know that. If people tell you things like that, they talk to you as if you were in Sunday school.

We would have asked him more, but it's better not to have things like that explained; Papa does not explain them. Mr. Evans made it seem clear and simple like that *Simple Science* that said everything in the wrong way. We do not have to have a book with a picture of a kettle on a kitchen fire to tell us what steam is.

But there are things that we must know. We must know why a nightmare is called a nightmare, but no one has yet explained it. He neighs like a horse when he laughs, he had a horse to ride when he was on the northern boundary which is that straight line on the map that separates us from Canada that he helped draw, that he had a dog team and Indian guides to help him with.

There was a dog with a barrel on his collar and a person asleep in the snow in our animal book; that was a Saint Bernard dog; the person was not dead, it looked like a girl with hair blown on the snow, but they said it was a boy who was asleep, not dead. You must not let yourself get warm in the snow; if you are terribly cold and then want to lie down and sleep because you feel happy and warm, you will freeze to death. The barrel had wine for the man in the snow. When he took us out to get that present, it was snowing. We walked down Church Street, then we turned down Main Street. Ida had put the top of the box down on the table and Gilbert was reaching in the box.

If the animals are there, then it did happen, then we did walk down Church Street, we three together, and we chose the animals.

Gilbert unwrapped the top animals; they were the Swiss wooden goat and the Swiss wooden bear that really were not for the *putz* but Mama kept them; then he said, "Here's your bear, Harold," and there it was.

It was the polar bear, and Gilbert of course remembered that it was Harold's. How could you forget how we had laid them all out on the floor, then had put them back in the box so as to see them all together, then had begun to choose?

Gilbert unwrapped the lion, he unwrapped the striped lynx that looked like a cat. He said, "I don't remember if this leopard is yours or Harold's." I said, "It's a lynx, it's mine."

I wondered if Papa remembered how he had bought the box of animals. Papa said, "Well, I must be off, *tempus fugit*," which were the letters written on the sundial that was still partly wrapped in its old sacking in the empty library. He let go my hand. I looked at him and saw that he was going.

✳ *BECAUSE ONE IS HAPPY*

Miss Helen let us draw on our slates, provided, she said, the drawings were not too silly.

Was a Christmas tree drawn on a slate, in and out of season, silly? It appeared not. Straight up, like the mast of a ship, then the branches in stark silhouette, a skeleton of a tree that looks bare; it looks really like a tent set up, with the down-sweeping branches for the tent folds or the crisscross of the twigs like the pattern on the tent, like Indians paint patterns on their tents. The tree indeed has come from the forest in which long ago there were Indians. There was an Indian who said the music coming from our church was the voice of the Great Spirit. That was when the Indians were coming down from the mountains one Christmas Eve. Everything happened—or should happen in our town—on Christmas Eve. Anyhow, this is all in a book; there were books with old pictures and drawings and photographs of our town. The Indians said, "It is the Voice of the Great Spirit," so the Great Spirit who was the Indian's God, was part of our God too; at least they went away. You draw the down-sweeping branches carefully, for if you make just silly scratches, Miss Helen says the drawing is not serious enough.

The thing is that you draw this tree, you rub it out with your damp sponge and polish off your slate with your bit of old towel that Ida has given you to keep in your school desk for your slate. Once in a while, Miss Helen tells whose slate-rags are too shabby. You get the sponges at John's, where you get slate-pencils and valentines and false faces for Halloween. You keep the sponge in a little saucer and make excuses to go to the washroom to wet the sponge, till Miss Helen says you must all do your sponges first thing in the morning or at recess. There may be a branch of chestnut, in water on the schoolroom windowsill, that has burst into heavy furry leaves. We do not draw the branch of the chestnut, but with the slightest lift of branches, this pine tree on a slate may be or could be a chestnut tree with its candlesticks of blossom.

This is magic against the evil that stings in the night. Its voice wails at two, at three (it is called the "siren" or the "alert") but safe, "frozen" in bed, there is magic. It is simple, innocuous magic. But sometimes through sheer nervous exhaustion, we drop off to sleep. We are not so safe then.

The serpent has great teeth, he crawled on Papa-and-Mama's bed and he was drinking water out of a kitchen tumbler, the sort of tumbler that we put our paintbrushes in. Then, I wonder why he is drinking water out of a common glass tumbler on Mama-and-Papa's bed. He does not spill the water. His great head is as wide as the tumbler but he drinks carefully and does not spill the water. Now I know there are three of us, I do not see their faces, but of course it is Harold and Gilbert.

The thing is, there is another snake on the floor, he may want water out of a glass, too; there is nothing very horrible about this until the snake on the floor rears up like a thick terrible length of fire hose around the legs of the bed. Then he strikes at me. I am not as tall as the footpiece of the bed, I could rest my elbows on the bed, like on a table. We spread out the *Arabian Nights* on Mama-and-Papa's bed and I said, "This is a girl," but Gilbert said, Aladdin was a boy. Was he? He wears a dress, he has long hair in a braid and a sort of girl-doll cap on his head. "Yes, yes," Ida says, "Aladdin is not a girl." Is it only a boy who may rub the wishing-lamp? I try it on the lamp on the stand in the parlor, but my wish does not happen, so maybe it is only a boy who may have the wish.

The snake has sprung at me and (though I know that Gilbert has been resting for a very long time, in a place called Thiacourt in France, and that Mama went to sleep too, in the early hours of the first day of spring long past, and did not wake up again) I shout through the snake-face, that is fastened at the side of my mouth, "Gilbert; Mama, Mama, Mama."

The snake falls off. His great head, as he falls away, is close to my eyes and his teeth are strong, like the teeth of a horse. He has bitten the side of my mouth. I will never get well, I will die soon of the poison of this horrible snake. I pull at Ida's apron but it is not Ida, it is our much-beloved, later, dark Mary. She looks at the scar on my mouth. How ugly my mouth is with a scar, and the side of my face seems stung to death. But no, "You are not stung to death," says dark Mary, who is enormous and very kind. "You must drink milk," she says. I do not like milk. "You must eat things you do not like," says Mary.

There is coal in our cellar and we have a washroom and Ida puts the washtubs on the bricks in the little outer-room that opens on to the garden. There is a great pear tree that has two kinds of pears because it has been grafted, and it has different kinds of pear blossoms. There is wisteria that grows up the side of the wash-kitchen.

"Can I help you wash clothes, Ida?" This is Ida, this is that mountain, this is Greece, this is Greek, this is Ida;

Helen? Helen, Hellas, Helle, Helios, you are too bright, too
fair, you are sitting in the darkened parlor, because you
"feel the heat," you who are rival to Helios, to Helle, to
Phoebus the sun. You are the sun and the sun is too hot for
Mama, she is sitting in the sitting room with Aunt Jennie
and they are whispering like they do, and they hide their
sewing when I come in. I do not care what they talk about.
They leave me out of everything. Ida does not leave me
out, "Here take this," says Ida. "Now squeeze it harder, you
can get it drier than that." I am helping Ida wring out the
clothes. Annie is wiping the soap from her arms from the
other washtub.

Mary came later, in the new house, with her little boy,
James.

But house is accordion-pleated on house and the dream
follows simple yet very subtle devices. We put Mary in the
old house and we can not reach beyond the band of her
apron where it is fastened round her waist. Mary, help us.
We must go further than Helen, than Helle, than Helios,
than light, we must go to the darkness, out of which the
monster has been born.

The monster has a face like a sick horrible woman; no,
it is not a woman. It is a snake-face and the teeth are pointed
and foul with slime. The face has touched my face, the
teeth have bitten into my mouth. Mary, pray for us. It is so
real that I would almost say an elemental had been conjured
up, that by some unconscious process my dream had left
open a door, not to my memories alone, but to memories of
the race. This is the vilest python whom Apollo, the light,
slew with his burning arrows.

This is the python. Can one look into the jaws of the
python and live? Can one be stung on the mouth by the
python and utter words other than poisonous? Long ago, a
girl was called the Pythoness; she was a virgin.

"What is a virgin, Mama?"

"A virgin is—is a—is a girl who isn't married."

"Am I a virgin, Mama?"

"Yes, all little girls are virgins."

All little girls are not virgins. The python took shape, his wings whirred overhead, he dropped his sulphur and his fire on us.

"Why did you cut out the picture from this book, Mama?"

"I—I—is it cut out?"

"Mama, someone cut out the picture from this book."

"What book, Sister?" She calls me Sister, but I am not her sister. She calls Aunt Aggie Sister, but Aunt Aggie and Aunt Laura are really her sisters. There are sisters in the Sisters' House and if I sing in the choir when I grow up, I will wear a cap and be one of the real Sisters. The Sisters open the big doors at the end of the church, when the church is dark on Christmas Eve and Papalie says *I am the light of the world* and the Sisters come through the two open doors with candles on trays. Then each of us has a candle with a different colored paper cut-out ruffle around the candle so that we do not spill the wax, which is beeswax and is made from the wax the bees get when they are getting honey from flowers.

I have not forgotten that she has cut out the picture, for no one else would dare cut out a picture from our book, from any book, with a pair of scissors.

"Why did you cut it out, Mama?"

"Oh—I—I thought you would forget."

Listen—it was a picture of—it was a picture of a nightmare. It was a picture of a little girl who was not married, lying on a bed, and a horrible creature that was like an old witch with snarling face, was riding on a stick, like a witch rides on a broomstick. She was going to stick the little girl right through with her long pointed stick and that was what would happen in the night if you went to sleep and had a bad dream which the *Simple Science* (which explains things like why does a kettle boil, which we do not have to have explained) calls a nightmare.

Look at its face if you dare, it is meant to drive you crazy. It is meant to drive you mad so that you fall down in a fit like someone in the Bible and see a light from heaven. It is terrible to be a virgin because a virgin has a baby with God.

The snow was not whirling round the lamppost when the old man sent his sleigh. The young man drove the horse; he was perched up on the seat, I sat with my back to him, Mama sat opposite with Gilbert on one side under the fur rug and Harold on the other. The snow lay very quiet, it did not whirl round the lampposts; it's made like stars, you can see them if you get them separate, if you get one stuck to the other side of the window; they have different shapes although there are so many that if you wrote 1 and then 000 forever, you would never write out a number, that would be the number of the snowflakes.

One snowflake shall not fall to the ground without your father.

But that was not a snowflake, that was a sparrow, but it means the same thing. Your father walks a little way; we wait under the light of the lamp that falls in a circle on the snow. I hold Harold's hand. He tugs at my hand, he does not say, "Why are you waiting?," but that is what he means when he pulls at my hand in my mitten, with this hand in his mitten. He does not speak very often. Mama says she is worried because Harold is so quiet. But Harold can talk. He is not dumb, he is a small child, he is a year younger than me. I hold his hand. He has on his new blue reefer. He wore a white coat only a little while ago, but now he wears a blue reefer.

Gilbert has gone ahead. That is our-father. No, I do not say that to Harold. I do not think it. I am so happy that

I am not saying anything, I am not thinking anything. I am alone by a lamppost, Harold has hold of my hand.

Our-father is half way between this lamp and the next lamppost, and Gilbert has run out in the road and is making a snowball.

If this was Mama or Aunt Jennie, taking us down Church Street, they would turn round, they would say, "Come along, children." He does not turn around. I will stand here by the lamppost because I am so happy. When you are too happy in the snow, Uncle Hartley told us, you might feel warm, you might think you were warm, then you might lie down in the snow and go to sleep, "So you children must race around in the snow." As if he had to tell us. We race around in the snow. But I am not warm, not warm enough to lie down on the snow like on a bed, yet I am warm. The light makes me warm, but not warm enough to lie down on the snow, which is dangerous, if you are too happy, like that man in the snow where the dog brings him a barrel on his collar. Papa will maybe turn round now but he does not, but Gilbert shouts, "Hi, you better catch up, you'll be late." He throws his snowball at the next lamppost but it does not hit the next lamppost. Papa does not say, "Hurry, come along," but on the Lehigh mountains he walks fast, so you have to run sometimes to catch up, but he does not say, "Don't get lost." He lets us get lost under the bushes and by the little stream when we go for pansy-violets and mayapples which have a white flower and two big leaves. The mayapple leaves are like an umbrella for the bunch of pansy-violets or the real violets we get.

It is not certain if he sees us. It is not certain if he knows that we are here.

Uncle Fred makes a doll out of the three corners of his handkerchief and it dances shadow-dances on the wall when he puts the lamp on the floor. Aunt Jennie threaded the smaller needle because the big needle was too thick to string the beads on. Indians have bead belts and moccasins. He walks ahead like an Indian who walks so quietly in the forest you do not hear him. Some boys (not the cousins) tied me to a post and played a game I do not remember. I know about it because Aunt Aggie told me how Gilbert rescued me from the strange boys in Aunt Aggie's street, before they moved to Washington; Aunt Aggie said, "He brought you in the house, and said, 'Aunt Aggie, will you take care of Sister, we are playing rough in the garden!' "

I can seem to remember being tied to a stake and wild Indians howling, and I do not know how soon they will strike at me with their tomahawks, but never in the snow.

Surely, I have not remembered this, only the lamppost stands there and Harold and I stand there and Gilbert is about to run back and say, "Come on, come on," he will rescue us, though we do not need to be rescued; we were never so happy, could never be happier. The light from the lamp is a round circle.

We wait in the snow, with the lamp, with Papa there, going on to the next lamppost, with Gilbert waiting to shout, though he pretends he is not thinking of us and stoops down to make another snowball.

It goes on in what we later called slow motion, at the moving-picture shows.

Or we stop there.

If we do not remember, it is nevertheless there. It crept up and its edge was white like the lamp, and the way it came up the flat sand was the way the snow drifts round the lamppost.

I was high up; his bathing suit was blue and stuck to his shoulders as we went together across the sand; he said, "No, it isn't cold, I'll take her in." He will take me in and that will be the end of me, but I am high up and the waves come close.

It is terrible to be taken in when the waves come up, but he does not drop me in.

He puts me down in the ocean. When the waves come up I run back and watch the waves come up after me, but it is a long way, the water goes on and on.

Mama does not like it. She does not like the hot sun; she sits under a parasol with Ida who is taking off Harold's white dress and putting bathing drawers on him. Gilbert is far away with some big boys and a boat.

"It is too far for you to walk," he told me.

There are pebbles, they are wet and shiny. There are shells.

Mama put the seashell to my ear and said, "Listen, you will hear the sea," but when we got to the sea it was too hot, she said, and she lay down in her room.

Professor Harding came with us. We ride down to the ocean in a big coach. Ida has a bag with towels and our bathing things.

"Come, come, don't be afraid." This is a boat and the boys are catching crabs; a crab is on the floor of the boat, he makes a horrible scratching on the wooden floor of the boat. There is a little square of water in the bottom of the boat but the boat won't sink, "Don't be afraid, girls are always afraid." Yes, I am afraid.

The crab comes along; you do not know which way he is walking, only that he is walking. He walks fast, fast. Girls are afraid. Don't scream. This is the worst thing that has ever happened. The crab gets bigger and bigger and the boys laugh more and more. "He won't eat you."

How do I know he won't eat me? The boat goes up and down with the waves and the crab opens his pincer-claws and one of the boys pushes him, even nearer. Then the crab comes nearer—girls scream sometimes.

"Here," says Papa and he picks up the crab with his

big hand and its claws grab round in the air and he is going to throw it back in the water.

"My crab," says Professor Harding who has on a big straw hat like a farmer. "Taking privileges with my property."

"Take your critter then," says Papa. He calls things a "critter," a crab or the alligator.

Professor Harding pushes a tub of water toward him, Papa drops the crab in the tub, the water splashes and the other critters claw round the edges of the tub.

When the alligator fell out of the attic window, the gardener screamed that it was the devil.

The gardener's name was Mr. Cherry.

"It can't be," said the Williamses, "you made it up."

"Mr. Cherry, Mr. Cherry," we called and he looked up, where he was tacking up a vine that has a purple flower that fell down. There was the bleeding-heart bush under the kitchen window, and above that was the window of Uncle Hartley's room where he slept in the afternoon, when he was at the steel mills the other side of the river at night. Then there was the little window above, just as you draw just the shape of such a house on a slate, when you do not draw the Christmas tree.

The alligator fell right into the bleeding-heart bush and the bush shook and waved, like blowing in the wind, and we knew what was there, but Mr. Cherry did not know and was surprised.

He ran away, but we did not.

We stood and watched the bush for the alligator to come out, but Uncle Hartley said, "You children better run off," but we did not because Papa was coming from the wash-kitchen door; he had on his big leather furnace-glove. He must have heard Mr. Cherry shriek or saw what happened, for he had on his big glove before Uncle Hartley could go back to the house and get whatever it was he was getting. I was glad it was not Papa's pistol. Then I thought, "I am glad he is not going to shoot the alligator."

He put his hand in the top of the bush and he had the alligator by the neck and he carried him into the house and up Papalie's front stairs past the clock, round the corner and up the next steps to the attic. Uncle Hartley tugged at the little attic window that was left open, and fastened it tight shut. "But you children better keep away from the attic," he said, "till we get some fresh wire nailed up here. Cherry will do it." Papa laughed like he does with a snort and said, "Better let me do it, Cherry doesn't like alligators."

Papa has a workbench in the little room beyond the kitchen over the wash kitchen where we keep our shoe-blacking and shoe brushes. He can make willow whistles.

Mamalie said, "St-st-st-st, that alligator better go."

We said and Tootie said and Dick stood watching, "Go where?"

"Well," said Mamalie, "after all . . ."

We said, "After all, what? Didn't someone send it to Papalie in a cigar box, wrapped in that Florida moss?"

Mamalie said, "Of course."

It is moss that we put under the tree for the animals to stand on and for the sheep to lie down in, and eat.

We made cherries out of cotton (like Papalie stuck on the clay sheep) for May Day, and Mrs. Williams trimmed Olive and Mea's leghorn hats with real tulips and leaves. Bessie had a crown of cherry blossoms on her hat, and when we had the May Day party in their garden under the cherry tree, Bessie was the queen because it was her birthday.

When we got home, Ida said, "Don't worry your mother, you can sleep in my bed tonight," and she woke me the next morning and her face was happy and she said, "Guess."

I said, "Guess what?"

She said, "You have a new brother."

I must have known all that, because we had talked about Mrs. Williams and the way she wore her raincoat all the time out-of-doors, even when it wasn't raining, and her wrapper indoors and Olive told me what it was, and then Amery came, but I did not seem to know. I seemed to be surprised. The baby was born on the second day of May.

Now at this minute, while we stand under the lamppost, he is not born yet, because he was born in May and this is Christmas and Harold is the baby.

Slow motion. Slower and slower.

Clock-time and out-of-time whirl round the lamppost. The snow whirls; it is white sand from the desert. Ahead is Papa, stopped in slow motion and then going back and back in time, back through the ages, the Middle Ages, though I do not know that, Rome, Greece; but he does not stop at Greece. The snow that has stopped in slow motion and folds us in a cloud is a pillar-of-cloud-by-day. The lamp shining over our heads is the pillar-of-fire, and the snow is the pillar-of-cloud and never, in-time or out-of-time, can such children be lost, for their inheritance is so great.

Gilbert must go to France, for Gilbert must inherit the pistol from Papa who was in our Civil War. Harold will inherit the mills and the steel and numbers too and become a successful businessman like Uncle Hartley. Gilbert has been asleep for a long time, in a place called Thiacourt, in France. Harold is a grown man, a grandfather with three children of his own; he inherited the three children, too, a girl and two boys. Hilda has inherited too much but she cannot let it go. There is the lamppost and the pillar-of-fire, and there is the cloud-by-day, the mystery, and Papa far ahead, a dark shape in the snow.

There was a hut in the woods, but the sun was shining, rain did not beat on the windows. He took us there to get water lilies.

A man with a horse and trap met us at the station. We were drawn toward a new scent, a new feel of trees, of light. It was evening.

As the daylight faded, there was new definition or exact understanding of twilight.

We had never been out in the woods in the evening.

Papa talked to the man who drove the horse, Papa had been here before; with whom? Not Mama. Had he brought those other children, Alfred and Eric and Alice (who was dead), here, before he married Mama? There was a world, a life of mystery beyond him; we could ask him about Indiana and how his father had gone out in a covered wagon and how frightened his mother was and how disappointed his father was to stay in Indiana because he wanted to go to California and how he himself had run away to go off with Alvin to the Civil War, and where did he find the Indian skull?

But we did not ask him what lay nearest, "Did you come here with Alfred and Eric and Alice who is dead. Did you come with their Mama?"

There was another mother, she was a mystery, she was dead, her name was Martha, we must not ask about her.

Here, the cart wheels went along a track just as wide as the wheels, for there was no road in the woods, only this opening in the trees that brushed Papa's head so that he had to duck his head, like going under a bridge in the canal boat when we took the canal boat and a picnic basket and a watermelon that Uncle Fred stopped to buy, on the way there.

Here there was no picnic basket, for we were going to spend the night in a place where we had never been, whose name was Sailor's Lake; "Is it a big lake?" asked Gilbert.

Papa snorted the way he did like a horse, when he laughed; he said, "It's a pond really."

A pond is a flat muddy waterhole where there are mosquitoes, back of the shanty-hill houses behind the mill where the goat once was, that Gilbert said looked like Papalie. But were we going to a shanty hill? We were going through a tunnel in the woods and the leaves brushed Papa's hat off and now he was holding his hat on his knees and looking up at the trees. Papa liked trees. He knew all about trees. We had a little chest of drawers he made, with little drawers and polished wood and brass handles to the drawers, that was too nice, Mama said, for me to use for my doll, but could I have it? Mama did not give it to me, but Mamalie gave me a little old chest that was hers, for my doll clothes.

The trees were deeper and maybe we were lost, but the man let the horse go along, he did not hold the reins, he was stuffing tobacco into his pipe. He offered Papa the tobacco and Papa laughed and said he had left his pipe in the pocket of his other coat, in the back of the cart; he said he liked a corncob pipe, too, best.

The horse was going to step on the little frogs.

"Stop the horse," I told Papa, "tell the man to stop the horse."

"Why?" said Papa.

"There is a little frog," and the man laughed and Papa laughed. He stopped the horse and told us to get out and there were a thousand-thousand little frogs on the track; they looked like small leaves fallen on the track until they began to hop.

"We can't help it," said the man, "if they get in the way, can we?"

We saw that the thousand-thousand little frogs lay like leaves on the track in the woods, that had two marks in it, just as wide as the wheels on the man's cart.

"Where is it?" we said. But then we saw from the porch, the way the field ran down along the side of the woods. There were no flowers along the edge of the porch, there was no wisteria, no climbing rose, no honeysuckle.

It was a hut in the woods.

There was the track from the wood-edge and marks where the cart stopped in front of the door. We came here last night. They said it was too late to run down to the lake.

"Then it is a lake?" said Gilbert.

"Of course," said the man.

It was a lake.

Here it was; we could not see how far it stretched because of the bulrushes, but there were boats tied to a wooden landing, so it must be a big lake. We ran back, up the slope of the field to the porch; there were no porch steps, the porch floor lay flat on the grass, the grass ran up to the floor of the porch; it was a house without a garden, the field was the lawn, the grass was long and short and you could see where the wheels of the cart stopped and went away again.

No one said, "Come along, come in to breakfast," but we went along and saw through the window that they were eating in the dining room. Papa was there at the table and the man who had the horse and an old lady and one or two others. They sat at a long table; there was a glass dish of pickled beets on the table and a pie and Papa was drinking coffee.

We saw Papa at a table without us, drinking coffee from a thick white cup.

We went in the hall and in the door to the dining room. Nobody said, "Where have you been?" The man-with-the-horse said, "Mother" to the door and the voice said, "Coming," and it was his mother we guessed or did he call his wife mother, like Papa called Mama sometimes? We could not tell if she was the cook or the man-with-the-horse's mother or his wife.

There were no children.

We sat along the table where there were places, not in a row.

The man-with-the-horse said, "Beets, pie, pickles?"

We said, "Yes."

Papa did not say, "You cannot have pie for breakfast."

We had pie for breakfast. It was huckleberry pie and we had napkins with red squares.

The coffee in Ida's house, when she took us to see her father-and-mother, smelt like this. But this was bigger than Ida's mother's-and-father's house and the windows were all open.

He did not come; he said yes, he would have more coffee.

We sat on the porch; I looked in the window and he was talking and laughing and everyone had gone but the man-with-the-horse, and they were smoking their pipes. The lady came in and put the cups on the tray; "Now he will come out," we thought, and he came out with his pipe and the man said, "Well, I better be off," and he knocked out the tobacco from his pipe on the railing of the porch, and he went off.

"Oh," he said and he came back, "Mamie leaks," and he laughed.

"Who is Mamie?" we said.

Papa said, "Come and see," and we ran down the grass, looking for Mamie. It was a boat, there was Lucy and Polly and Mamie; Papa read out the names and said, "Which do you want?" and we said, "Polly."

Polly is the name of a parrot. Aunt Jennie had a Polly that ate crackers, or you said, "Polly have a cracker," and if it said, "Polly have a cracker," back at you, we gave it some sunflower seeds. The sunflower seeds are like little nuts if you bite into them.

Papa took the two oars. The oars caught in the bulrushes, everywhere there were bulrushes; we were caught here and the sun was shining.

We waited for Papa to put back the oars in the boat, and he pulled the boat along by the bulrushes; then I saw what it was we had come to see. It spread back and it was bigger than a white rose.

"Stop, stop," I said, though the boat was going slowly.

"What is it?" said Papa.

"Look," I said, and Harold looked and Gilbert looked.

"The boat will run over it," I said. I was in the front of the boat and Gilbert was in the back with the two ropes for the rudder. Harold crawled along.

"Is it a naligator?" he said.

I said, "No, you know they come from Florida. It's gone, Papa you have run over it."

Papa said, "What?"

He went on pulling the boat along by the bulrushes.

It was gone. I would never see it again, it would be squashed and dead, it would be torn up by the boat. I wanted the boat to go back.

Papa said, "What was it?"

I said—I said—but I could not speak because now he had pulled the boat out and given it a push with the oars, and I saw what it was that we had come to see.

There was not just one water lily there on the water, like the one we had run over. They were crowded together so that sometimes one was pushed sideways, like our pears when there are too many on a branch. They were under my hands when I reached out.

"Don't fall in," said Papa.

I saw the picture in our Hans Andersen about Peter the child, or was it Peter the stork?

There is a story in our Hans Andersen about a stork and children. The babies like the innocents in our Doré Bible wait there on the water lilies.

It was not that I thought of the picture; it was that something was remembered. There was a water lily, painted on blue velvet, in Mrs. Kent's house, but she said it was not stylish any more to have painting on velvet. But it was very pretty. There were bulrushes, painted on a blue umbrella-stand. It seemed that the water lilies, painted on the velvet and the blue umbrella-stand with bulrushes painted on it, were not in my mind, any more than the picture of the water lilies lying large and flat-open on the pond or lake in the Hans Andersen story.

They were not at first there, but as the boat turned round and shoved against the bulrushes and then the bul-rushes got thinner and you could see through them (like looking through the slats in a fence), you saw what was there, you knew that something was reminded of something. That something remembered something. That something came true in a perspective and a dimension (though those words, of course, had no part in my mind) that was final; nothing could happen after this, as nothing had happened before it, to change the way things were and what people said and "What will you do when you grow up" and "It must be exciting to have so many brothers" or "You've torn a great triangle in your new summer dress and the first time you wore it, too" (as if I did not know that) or "That branch of the pear tree is dead, be careful when you children climb that tree," but it was not us but Teddie Kent who fell out of it, because he said, "The old thing is no deader than the rest of the old tree," and climbed out, just because we said, "Don't," and fell down and broke his arm.

And Jack Kent ran away and was gone a whole night, and when he came back Mrs. Kent cried, and that seemed a funny thing to do, "Why did she cry, Mama?"

"Well, she cried with relief, because she was so happy."

"Can one cry because one is happy, Mama?"

✳ *THE SECRET*

The stars?

"Well—there's a . . ." and the voice stops, and they all stop talking. This is later in the new house. They are sitting under my window. I am in bed, they are under the window. *My garden is under the window* was in our first entertainment at the old school; I mean, they were my words to speak. They had made a window at the back of the platform, and we stood together in a row; we were from Kate Greenaway. I was in the middle with two boys, but the boys were in my first class at school and we were all six years old and they were not my brothers.

But this is the new house. They are sitting on the grass. They pulled their chairs out from under the big maple tree. It is summer, and they come to see us; Uncle Fred and Aunt Jennie are staying with us. Mamalie is here too, but she is not a visitor. *"My"* someone else is there but it does not matter who it is. I think Mamalie has gone to bed, too. I wonder if she hears them say *"my,"* then I seem to know what they are looking at, why they have stopped talking.

They always have so much to say; Uncle Hartley and Aunt Belle come too, but Aunt Jennie and Mama laugh most. Maybe that is Cousin Ed saying "It reminds me of. . . ." They always say it reminds them of. Papa is at the transit house, Eric is at the observatory looking for his double stars. The double stars stay together, but they go round one another like big suns; we know this, for he tells the visitors at the observatory Thursday evenings and we tell them to sign their names in the visitor's book. This is not Thursday. You can almost tell what day of the week it is by the feel of something in the air, but it was easier to tell in the old town because of the church bells and the factory whistles, the other side of the river. Uncle Hartley is going to get a promotion and go to another place than Bethlehem Steel. They will have a new house like our new house when we came here and Papa left his little observatory for this new transit house, which has the only instrument (except in Greenwich, England) like he has. Mr. Evans lives in the wing of the house, and Eric has his room in the wing of the house over the empty library, but they are bringing out maps and books now for the observatory library from the university library.

"The first this year—the first real one, I mean . . ."

Mamalie is not in bed. She is coming up the stairs. The clock is ticking. It has a loud tick. Maybe she has forgotten her knitting, maybe I will run downstairs and get her knitting for her in the dark. The house is dark because the mosquitoes come in even though we have new screens on all the windows. "Mamalie," she is at the top of the stairs now.

"Mamalie. . . ."

"What—what—is that you, Helen?" She calls me "Helen" sometimes and she calls Harold "Hartley," but we do not say, "My name is not Helen" or "My name is not Hartley," we just answer.

"Mamalie. . . ."

"Yes—yes, Helen—what is it?"

"It's me, Mamalie. . . ."

"Oh—it's you."

"Mamalie. . . ."

"Yes—yes—Laura, I mean Helen—Oh, Hilda, of course, what is it?"

"Did you forget your knitting?"

"Why—yes—yes, I think I left my knitting on the window seat in the sitting room."

"Shall I run down for it?" I am out of bed now. I stand by her in the dark in the hall, at the top of the stairs. Their voices go on outside. ". . . when we hired the old post-coach, for fun—do you remember? We clubbed together for Uncle Sylvester's birthday treat and drove to the Water Gap and . . ." They are all there, and what they said *"ah"* about is a shooting star, and Aunt Jennie says you can make a wish on your first shooting star.

I did ask Eric why it was called a shooting star and he said because it streaks or shoots across the sky—"But would it fall on us?" He said no, there was something about gravity that would keep it from falling, but how do they know that? I did not ask silly questions like the visitors Thursday evenings at the observatory who say, "Are there people on Mars?," but sometimes I wonder if they are able to tell if really a shooting star will not fall down and fall on us and fall on the house and burn us all to death. It is quiet now.

"Mamalie. . . ."

"Why aren't you asleep, Laura?"

"Oh, I don't know—they're talking outside."

"That's no reason not to go to sleep, they always sit on the porch or on the lawn and talk when it's so hot."

"Yes—because if they light the lamp the June bugs bump in."

". . . but you're shivering."

"It's only goose-flesh, Mamalie," I say. I don't quite know what I mean by goose-flesh, but I just say something to keep her standing in the dark.

"And why do they call it goose-flesh, Mamalie?" though I know that, too; it's because if you're cold you get little rough pimples like a goose has when it is in its dish waiting for the oven, but the roughness doesn't really look much like goose-flesh; it's like that thing they call your-hair-standing-on-end, but it doesn't really. But I have asked her one quick question which she hasn't answered, so if I am able, I will ask her another. I reach out and the wall is there and it is a hot night and I am cold. "Why do they call a shooting star, a shooting star, Mamalie?"

"Well . . . I—I suppose because—"

"It might hit a house, mightn't it? I mean, it might shoot down and hit us?"

"Why should it?" She is brushing past me as if I were not there. She must not do that.

"Mamalie. . . ." I feel along the wall. "Where are you going, Mamalie?" She does not answer. She is like that. Sometimes she does not answer, she does not look up when she is knitting, she even sits without her knitting and is not asleep, but "Don't disturb your grandmother," Mama will say. It is not just because she is getting a little deaf in one ear, but we know which ear that is and stand on the side of her "good ear," as she calls it. But she is hearing something all the same; you can see that she is hearing something. Maybe she is hearing something now in the dark. I have forgotten about the shooting star. Maybe she will let me stay in her room. If I stay in her room with her, I might hear something.

She is feeling for the matches in her top bureau drawer. She has her lace caps there and handkerchiefs in sachet, and there is cologne on the top of her bureau.

"They're in the left corner, at the back," I prompt her, "you told me to remind you if you forgot." She hides the matches in different corners, as if she were afraid of them. But she has found the matches. She strikes a match, and there is a little flame from the candle in a saucer; she keeps a saucer and the candle standing on the top of her bureau.

She will put the saucer on a chair by her bed. It is a night light, and she will even ask me sometimes to pour water in the saucer from her pitcher on the washstand, and then we have to pour some out again, because it is too much for the candle, and then we get it just right, so that the candle will go out and not set anything on fire if it starts to sputter. She even carries a candle in the train, in her handbag, in case, she says, "the lights should all go out in a tunnel"

"But do they?"

"Do they what, Aggie?" Now she is calling me "Aggie." I wonder if she will notice, she never calls me "Aggie," but why shouldn't she call me "Aggie" if she calls me "Helen" or "Laura" even? Now I am Aggie; this is the first time I have been Aggie. I stand in my nightdress and see the room, and it is a different room and I am Aggie. It is summer I know, but I do not hear their voices because Mamalie's room is this side of the house, away from the front steps and the grass where we have the new little magnolia tree planted.

She will never unpin her cap because she has a little bald spot on the top of her head, she says, but now she un-pins her cap. I see Mamalie without her cap and she looks just the same, only maybe not so old because the light is not very bright and her hair is not all-over white but partly white, and where it is not white you can see that it is black, but very black, not like Mama's, or mousy as they call mine.

Her eyes slant up at the sides, yes, you can see now that she looks like Aunt Aggie, only Aunt Aggie is a taller lady, taller than Mama even. It seems that it is cold, though it is a hot summer night, but there is wind this side of the house because the curtains blow a little in the wind, and I can see that Mamalie is afraid they'll brush against the candle in the saucer, even before she says, "The curtains, Aggie."

I go over and jerk the summer curtains; they are made of flowered stuff, like the curtains they pinned up for the window they cut out of an old screen that they stood up for a house in a garden when I was *My garden is under the window*. It was that kind of window curtain, and this had little daisies and wild roses running along and little yellow flowers in the corner that Mama said were English primroses and grow wild in England, but we had not seen them, only the ones that grow bunched on a stem that the Williamses had in their garden, that Mrs. Williams called "primulas" and that Mamalie called "keys-of-heaven."

It is better to get in her bed. It is not cold, but the quilt she always brings with her in her trunk is pretty; it is made of patches of everybody's best dresses and some French stuff that was sent by one of the old-girls from New Orleans. Mamalie can tell me about the dresses; I will want to ask her again about this black one with the tiny pink rosebuds, that was one of Aunt Aggie's to go to Philadelphia in, when she married Uncle Will. I can pull up the quilt and I can sit here and I am not afraid now to think about the shooting star because I think she is going to talk about the shooting star in a different way that isn't gravitation.

She said, "I forgot all about it."

I don't know if that is the shooting star or the question I am thinking of asking her (because sometimes she seems to know what I am going to ask her and answers me beforehand) about Aunt Aggie's black silk dress with rosebuds, but she has not forgotten about that because she was telling me about it only the other day when I helped her unpack. She will stay as long as she can, but then she must get back to Bethlehem; it will be for one of those things, like putting flowers on Papalie's grave for his birthday or the day he died on, but she seems to like to be with us here and goes in the kitchen and makes Papa apple pies. Now she has pulled out the bone hairpins that she wears at the top, to keep up her braids. She has two braids, and they hang down now, either side of her face, and she might almost be a big girl or a little girl sitting in the low chair with the candle on the window sill.

"I would have told you before but I forgot, Agnes."

I say, "Yes, Mimmie," because Mama and Aunt Aggie call her "Mimmie." I am afraid she will remember that I am only Hilda, so I crouch down under the cover so she will only half see me, so that she won't remember that I am only Hilda.

"It wasn't that I was afraid," she said, "though I was afraid. It wasn't only that they might burn us all up, but there were the papers. Christian had left the secret with me. I was afraid the secret would be lost."

I do not know who Christian is and I am afraid to ask. Or does she mean a Christian? It is the same name as Hans Christian Andersen. I get tired of hearing them talk about the picture someone called Benjamin West painted of a lady called Mary Ann Wood (I think her name was) and the spinet that the fan-maker in London gave to someone; anyhow their grandfather had a spinet in his house, even if it wasn't that one, and that would be Mamalie's papa, why yes, that would be Mamalie's own papa, and perhaps Mamalie played the spinet, though she never plays the piano.

Now it seems that I can understand why they are so interested in Mary Ann Wood and what she had, because all at once I understand about the spinet, and I even wonder about the fan-maker in London and who he was and who he made fans for and what the fans were like and why did he give the spinet away and did they bring it with them on the same boat or did they send it on another boat and what was the name of the ship they came on, anyway?

For the first time in my life, I wonder who we all are? Why, Mamalie's own Mama was called Mary and she was from Virginia, and her father and mother had come straight from Scotland, and I did not even know their names nor the name of the ship they came on. Mamalie's own mama's name was Mary, and is that why (I wonder for the first time) Mamalie always gets Uncle Fred to sing *The Four Marys* the last thing after Thanksgiving or Christmas parties?

I never thought about who they were very much, and anyhow I could always find out by asking them, but now for the first time I really want to know; I want to know who Christian is, because somehow Christian is not one of the ones Mama and Uncle Hartley and Cousin Ed talk about, but Christian is someone I just hear about, alone with Mamalie, as if Christian belonged alone to me and Mamalie, and didn't she say, anyhow, there was a secret?

"Christian," I say half to myself, because I cannot help it though I have not meant to ask her about Christian, because Aunt Aggie perhaps knew all about him, but Mamalie might come back and remember that I am Hilda and that I am not Agnes. But I did not say "Christian" very loud, perhaps she did not hear me.

Mamalie came back, she looked round the room, she said, "What was I saying, Hilda?"

I said, "I was thinking of asking you about this scrap, it's black with pink rosebuds; Aunt Aggie said is was a silver-grey dress that she had for Philadelphia when she married Uncle Will."

Mamalie said, "You said something, or somebody said something, who said something?"

I said, "It's you and me, Mamalie, I was asking about Aunt Aggie, I was thinking about—about—church—I mean,

I was thinking about something. . . ." Mamalie puts her hand up to her hair, she presses her hands against the sides of her face as if to hide the two long braids that have white threads in them but look darker when they are down than when they are looped up either side of her face, under her lace cap.

"What were you talking about before I went to sleep?" said Mamalie. I do not tell her that she has not been asleep.

"We were talking—because I heard them talking—I was cold." What will I say now? "It's too dark to read to me, Mamalie," I say, "but I was thinking I'd ask you to read. I was thinking, I'd get my new fairy tales. I don't know, I may have said out aloud—you know how it is—'I'll get my new fairy tales, I'll get Hans Christian Andersen.' "

I said again, "I'll get Hans Christian Andersen."

"They were talking outside the window," I said, "I was listening to them and they said "ah." They were saying "ah" because it was a shooting star. Aunt Jennie says you can have a wish on your first summer shooting star. I did not think of any wish, anyhow I did not see it, I only heard them talking. I wished, if I wished anything, that I would not think it might fall on the house. I knew it could not, because of gravity or something like that, that keeps the stars from falling on us and keeps the world going round. Gravity keeps the earth on its track, and Mr. Evans explained about Papa in the transit house. Eric is in the observatory, looking at his double stars."

"Double stars," said Mamalie.

"I heard you coming up the stairs, and I said, could I get your knitting and you said no, I think, or maybe you didn't answer at all, and then we lit the candle."

"Yes," said Mamalie, "we lit the candle."

"Then you took off your cap." She puts up her hand, she is feeling for her cap. I wonder why she thinks she must always wear a lace cap?

"I wanted one of the little tight caps," she said, "like the early Sisters wore, and I wanted to be one of the single Sisters but Christian said it was best not, because already the German reformed people were accusing us of popish practices."

I said, "What are popish practices, Mamalie, and who is Christian?"

She said, "I thought you knew, Agnes, that I called your father Christian."

She said *Gnadenhuetten,* and it does not matter what it is or where it is or what it means or anything about it. It is the same when Papa calls me *Töcterlein,* it simply makes everything quite different, so that sometimes I am sure that I am really in the woods, like when Mama plays *Träumerei* which isn't very good music, she says, but I ask her to play it because it's called *Träumerei.*

It would be no good my trying to learn German because, when I look at one of the German grammar books in the bookshelves, it stops working. A row of words called *der–die–das* doesn't belong to it. I would rather talk German, real German, than anything. I do not want to learn German, I do not even want them to know how much I feel when they say *Gnadenhuetten* like that. I am in the word, I am *Gnadenhuetten* the way Mamalie says it, though I do not know what it means.

"And *Wunden Eiland,*" she says.

It seems as if something had come over me like the branches of a tree or the folds of a tent when she says *Wunden Eiland.* She says *Eiland* which must be an island, and the

Wunden, I suppose, is wonder or wonderful. I do not even want her to tell me, but I want her to go on talking because if she stops, the word will stop. The word is like a beehive, but there are no bees in it now. I am the last bee in the beehive, this is the game I play. The other bees have gone, that is why it is so quiet. Can one bee keep a beehive alive; I mean, can one person who knows that *Wunden Eiland* is a beehive, keep *Wunden Eiland* for the other bees when they come back?

But it won't be any use just thinking like this, because if I don't say something, she might really go to sleep, or she will talk the whole thing out in German and I don't want to listen to her talking nothing but German, because then I start to think about it, and if I start to think about it, it gets *der–die–das*-ish and I am angry that I cannot understand or that I cannot learn it quickly. But *Wunden Eiland* is not a thing you learn, it's not a thing that anyone can teach you, it just happens.

"Tell me more about the island," I say, though maybe *Eiland* isn't an island, though I think it must be.

"It was washed away," said Mamalie.

Mamalie is talking like something in a book and I do not very much understand what she is saying. I have heard of Count Zinzendorf, of course, who founded the *Unitas Fratrum,* the United Brethren which is our Church or which was our Church before we moved from Bethlehem.

Unitas Fratrum is united brethren, like United States is united states, and they have a sign which is a lamb, like the United States has an eagle, and they have a flag with a cross. Mamalie says it is a flag the crusaders used or a banner, but that was long ago, only it is all long ago.

I think four hundred years back; it is because we all had a holiday when it was 1892, which was four hundred years since Columbus discovered America. But the *Unitas Fratrum* seemed to have discovered something which was very important, that was in Europe. They came to America to bring the secret from Europe or to keep the secret to themselves. But something happened like it always does, it seems, so that the United Brethren weren't really united.

Mamalie said, "My Christian explained the secret to me; it seemed very simple to me. It was simply belief in what was said—*and, lo, I am with you alway, even unto the end of the world.* You see, those words were taken literally."

There were all these questions in a row, each with its particular question mark. I did not think them out nor see them in writing, but some of them were:

Did you play the spinet, Mamalie? Did you play *Four Marys?*

Who were the four Marys, and why were there four?

Who has our Grimm, and did they lose the picture of the Princess and the Frog, that was loose and partly torn across?

Why are they all called Christian or does it just mean that they are Christian?

Why do they make it a secret, because anybody can read what it says in the Bible, *lo, I am with you alway?*

Did great-grandfather Weiss like Christian Henry more than he liked Francis, who is Mama's own father?

Why do you always think there might be a fire or didn't you, was it me or Mama thought it?

Why are you frightened and put your hand to your hair? (I want long hair, but if an Indian came to scalp you, perhaps it would be worse.)

What were the papers?

"What were the papers, Mamalie?" I said.

Now Mamalie told this story which I did not altogether understand but pieced together afterwards—I mean long afterwards, of course, because the "thing" that was to happen, that was in a sense to join me in emotional understanding, in intuition anyway, to the band of chosen initiates at *Wunden Eiland,* had not yet happened.

The "thing" that was to happen, happened soon afterwards, maybe that very autumn or winter. It was before Christmas, say in November, or it was after Christmas was well over, say in February, but I cannot date the time of the thing that happened, that happened to me personally, because I forgot it. I mean it was walled over and I was buried with it. I, the child was incarcerated as a nun might be, who for some sin—which I did not then understand—is walled up alive in her own cell or in some anteroom to a cathedral.

It was as if I were there all the time, in understanding anyway, of the "thing" that had happened before I was ten, the "thing" that had happened to me and the "thing" I had inherited from them. I, the child, was still living, but I was not free, not free to express my understanding of the gift, until long afterwards. I was not in fact, completely free, until again there was the whistling of evil wings, the falling of poisonous arrows, the deadly signature of a sign of evil magic in the sky.

The same fear (personal fear) could crack the wall that had originally covered me over, because to live I had to be frozen in myself—so great was the shock to my mind when I found my father wounded. I did not know, as Mamalie began talking, that *Wunden Eiland* was Island of the Wounds; it came clear afterwards. Bits of it came clear, as I say, in patches; the story was like the quilt that I drew up to my chin, as I propped myself up in her bed, to listen.

Roughly, a hundred years had passed, since the founding of the town and the rituals practiced at *Wunden Eiland,* which, Mamalie had explained, was actually an island in the Monocacy River which, in Mama's day, was called a creek, though it could occasionally break its boundaries in the season of floods, as that time Mama told us about, when the deer that Papalie had in the seminary grounds were lost.

A hundred years had passed, since the founding of the town I mean, when Mamalie's Christian found the papers or the scroll of flexible deerskin which told the story of the meeting of the chief medicine men of the friendly tribes and the devotees of the Ritual of the Wounds. Christian, who was no mean scholar, glimpsed here a hint in Hebrew or followed a Greek text to its original, and so pieced out the story of the meeting, deciphered actually the words of strange pledges passed, strange words spoken, strange rhythms sung which were prompted, all alike said, by the power of the Holy Spirit; the Holy Ghost of the Christian ritualists and the Great Spirit of the Indians poured their grace alike; their gifts came in turn to Anna von Pahlen, to John Christopher Frederick Cammerhof, to John Christopher Pyrlaeus, who was not only a scholar and authority on the Indian languages, but a musician as well.

Well, where had Mamalie's gift gone then? I did not ask her, but I sense now that she burnt it all up in an hour or so of rapture, that she and her young husband together recaptured the secret of *Wunden Eiland;* and not only the secret, but the actual Power that had fallen on Anna and Zeisberger and Paxnous and Morning Star, fell, a hundred years afterwards, on the younger Christian Seidel and his wife, Elizabeth Caroline, who was our grandmother. As Mamalie outlined it, it seemed that, in trying over and putting together the indicated rhythms, she herself became one with the *Wunden Eiland* initiates and herself spoke with tongues—hymns of the spirits in the air—of spirits at sunrise and sunsetting, of the deer and the wild squirrel, the beaver, the otter, the kingfisher, and the hawk and eagle.

She laughed when she told me about it, so I know that she and Christian (or Henry) who was Aunt Agnes' father, must have been very happy.

We are back at the beginning. This is just a bedroom. Why, I am sitting up in Mamalie's bed, and there were voices outside my window. *My garden is under the window* is the first line of a poem that I recited, the first time I recited anything on a stage. It was a large audience, they clapped, and Miss Helen said I must go out and be out of the window and make a bow. I made a bow. Now, this is something like that. They were acting something.

Mamalie has forgotten that she was not at *Wunden Eiland;* she said, "The laughter ran over us," but she was a hundred years later, and she just picked out notes (that she had carefully looked up in the hymnbooks and in the old folios) that John Christopher Pyrlaeus had indicated to her, down the side of a page. Mamalie must be very clever. She never told me about this. She never, I know, told anyone about this. And now she is telling me about it. It is as if she had been there at that meeting, only she couldn't have been there. How does she know that they laughed?

There was a seal that had a cup and an S on it. The S was for *Sanctus Spiritus* that means the Holy Ghost that nobody seems to understand, but that Mamalie said that Anna von Pahlen and John Christopher Frederick Cammerhof found at a meeting at *Wunden Eiland;* that was a scandal. What is a scandal?

It was a blot on the church, they said, and they didn't have any meetings like that anymore, and Mamalie says that Christian—her Christian—found that they had made a pact or a pledge, but it was in the spirit, in the *Sanctus Spiritus,* and it seems they didn't keep it. They couldn't keep it because the stricter Brethren of the church said it was witchcraft. What exactly is witchcraft? You can be burnt for a witch. Is Mamalie a witch? She is crouching over the candle, she is holding the saucer with the candle in it in her hand. What is Mamalie saying to the candle?

". . . *until the Promise is redeemed and the Gift restored.*"

But she said that before. She said that when she was telling me about the copy of the promise that they made to one another, that was written on deerskin, or maybe it was parchment. They made a promise, but it was not Mamalie's fault if they did not keep the promise; how could it be? I suppose the gift was their all talking and laughing that way and singing with no words or with words of leaves rustling and rivers flowing and snow swirling in the wind, which is the breath of the Spirit, it seems.

Mamalie helped her husband who was named Henry, but she called him Christian, or maybe his name was Henry Christian—anyhow, he was dead. I mean, he was dead almost from the beginning, because Aunt Aggie was not a year old, I think, when he died. Morning Star was the Indian Princess who was the wife of Paxnous, who was baptized by the Moravians. She was really baptized, it seems; Paxnous was not baptized, but the Indians took Anna von Pahlen into their mysteries in exchange for Morning Star. I mean, Anna was Morning Star in their mysteries, and Morning Star (who had another ordinary Indian name like White-cloud or

Fragrant-grass or one of those names) was Angelica which was another name of Anna von Pahlen, who was really Mrs. John Christopher Frederick Cammerhof, but I like to think of her as Anna von Pahlen.

Mamalie is talking to the candle. Really, it is not her fault.

"It is not your fault," I say.

I am sure it is not her fault, whatever it is. Maybe she was afraid they would burn her for a witch (like they did at Salem, Massachusetts) if she told them that she could sing Indian songs, though she didn't know any Indian languages, and that she and her Christian had found out the secret of *Wunden Eiland* which, the church had said, was a scandal and a blot.

Maybe it was all shadows and pictures in Mamalie's mind, maybe there never was a parchment, maybe there never was such a meeting at *Wunden Eiland,* maybe there never was a *Wunden Eiland.*

"Maybe there never was a *Wunden Eiland,*" I say.

"What—what," she says, "Lucy."

Now, who is Lucy? Is that old Aunt Lucia that we used to take sugar cake to, at the Widows' House?

"I told you it was all written, I told you the parchment was—was—Lucy, water," says Mamalie and she seems to be choking. Now I am frightened. "Lucy," she says, "someone must find the papers, someone must work out the music, now Christian is dead. Lucy," she says, "who can do the work—who can follow the music? Music, Lucy," she says. Now I am frightened. I put one foot out of bed. I get out of bed; I walk round the bed. I stand looking at Mamalie. I take the candle from her hand.

"Be still," I say, "be still, it's all right." I do not call her Mamalie, I do not even call her Mimmie. "It's all right," I say, "it's all right, Elizabeth."

I think this is a good idea to call her Elizabeth, though it rather frightens me. If she thinks I am Lucy, then I am not Agnes any more, and if I am not Agnes, she is not Mimmie any more. I think it must be old Aunt Lucia she is talking to, at the Widows' House, who died.

Ida used to put an apple pie or a sugar cake in a basket with a clean napkin over the top, and Gilbert would carry the basket and we would take the sugar cake or the apple pie to Aunt Lucia. Mamalie says "Lucy," but I think this is old Aunt Lucia who wasn't an aunt at all, but we have many aunts, and Mama has many aunts who were sisters in the church to Mamalie, so I suppose they were aunts to us, in the church.

It is all about the church. It is something the church thought was bad and Mamalie was part of it, though she wasn't really, because it was a hundred years earlier, but she said, when she played the songs, it all came back. Songs bring things back like that, it seems. Did she sing the songs? I never heard her sing. I don't think Mama ever heard her sing. She asks me to sing *Abide with me* and Mama plays the tune for it; Mamalie always asks me to sing; I think she is the only person who always asks me to sing.

She asks me to sing *Fast falls the eventide. The darkness deepens.* She is always afraid, it seems, in the dark, and she asks me to sing *The darkness deepens.* It's not really dark in this room, but then I am not afraid of the dark. I am afraid more of a bright light that might be fire and a shooting star falling on the house and burning us all up.

It all started with the shooting star and my asking questions.

But I must do something, she might come back in a hurry and wonder where she is. But it might be better if she did come back because where she is, she is thirsty, and she talks about the parchment being burnt and herself being burnt and the promise and the penalty if they didn't keep the promise, and about great wars and the curse on the land, if we did not keep the promise, and how Morning Star was the soul God gave the church and the church did not recognize Morning Star, even though the *morning stars sang together*. But they didn't. The morning stars didn't sing together, she said; she said, "Shooting Star, Shooting Star, forgive us," and something about a curse and things like that. I really did not know what to do. I was glad she was talking quietly, almost whispering, for I would not have liked it if Mama had burst in or Aunt Jennie, laughing and joking and saying, "What—what—you two not in bed yet?"

I remember that Aunt Aggie did say that Mamalie was very sick, and while Mamalie had that bad fever, she was sent to stay with old Auntie Bloom for over a year, and Aunt Aggie called Auntie Bloom "Mimmie" too; Aunt Aggie thought Auntie Bloom was her own mother, for a long time, she said. I suppose this is it. Aunt Aggie is now living with Auntie Bloom, and she is a very tiny little girl and I am not Aggie any more, but I am Aunt Lucy or Aunt Lucia, and I suppose I am nursing Mamalie because the Moravian Sisters made medicines and had patches of old gardens with mint and sage and things they made into medicines.

I am the nurse of Mamalie who is very ill and had some sort of fever, maybe brain fever, they said; anyhow I think it is very sad that she was afraid (when she had her fever) that Shooting Star was angry with her.

She said she was thirsty; I wonder if it wouldn't be a

good idea to get her a glass of water from the washstand and pretend to be Lucy and try to get her to go to bed? I go to the washstand. The washstand jug is nearly full of water, and it is very heavy. It would be terrible if I dropped the pitcher: this is a jug or a pitcher, like the *seidel* that was the cup with the S, that was *Sanctus Spiritus,* that was the sign of the communion so that the old uncle turned it into an urn and put the S on a shield, Mamalie said, but Mamalie said he had the same words in French, *l'amitié passe même le tombeau.*

Now it seems, while I pour out water from the pitcher into the glass, that I am Hilda pouring out water from a wash-stand jug that has roses and a band of dark blue that looks like a painted ribbon round the top. The tooth-mug matches the pitcher. There is a soap dish with a little china plate, with holes in it, that is separate so that the water from the soap will drip through. The basin has the same roses.

The pitcher is heavy, but I do not spill the water.

The quilt has pulled off the bed where I got out.

The water seems cool enough. I put down the jug any-how, and now I take the heavy glass up and feel the outside, and it is not so very cool, and I remember it is a hot night. Now I am not cold, and I remember it is a hot night. I could go to the pantry and get some cracked ice, but that will be a little trouble, and the others will be sure to burst in and say, "Why aren't you in bed" and spoil everything.

I walk round the quilt that is partly spread on the floor, and I do not step on the patch that was Aunt Sabina's moiré or old Cousin Elizabeth's watered silk. I must remember that Mamalie is just Elizabeth, not old Cousin Elizabeth, and I get round the bed, and she is sitting there and the candle is there in the saucer and the curtain is hanging straight and there is no sort of wind. I remember there was a wind that rattled the curtain rings, but there is no wind, and if I listen, I can begin to hear footsteps and their dragging the chairs up the porch steps from the grass like they always do, in case it rains in the night. I had thought there might be a thunder-storm because Mama says on very hot nights, "It feels thun-der–y." It had been feeling thunder–y, though that is per-haps not what it was; I mean, it was what you mean when you say your hair stands on end, though it doesn't really. But that was, maybe, the best part of it, like listening to a ghost story at a party in the dark.

It was like listening in the dark, though we had the candle, and maybe it was just a story in the dark with a candle, about something that didn't happen at all, like the ghost story about the man who nailed his coat to a coffin and then screamed because he thought a skeleton hand had got him. Only this was something different, though I couldn't tell just how, only that it made Mamalie shiver and then say that about Shooting Star forgiving them or something. I think maybe it was a sort of dream, maybe it did not happen. Maybe, even, I made it up alone there on the bed while Mamalie was sitting at the window; maybe, Mamalie didn't even say anything at all; maybe it is like that time when I saw the old man on Church Street and he sent his sleigh and Mama said it never happened. Maybe it is like that thing that happened, that Mama said didn't happen, when the young man, who at first I thought was the gardener, cut off or broke off a lily with a short stem that I held in my hand like a cup. Maybe. . . .

I think if I just take the glass and hand it to Mamalie and she just says, "Thank you, Helen," or "Thank you, Hilda," then it will be that I was asleep or half-asleep on the

bed and that I dreamed all this and that maybe, I did, after
all, only dream about the old man and the drive in the snow
when all the streets were empty, when we drove past our
house on Church Street and Mama sat opposite me with
Harold and Gilbert under the fur rug and the man, who at
first I thought was the gardener, sat up in front and drove
the horses.

Maybe, that was just a dream, and maybe the lily with
the short stem that I held in my hands like a cup, was some-
thing I dreamed, just as maybe I dreamed that Mamalie said
that our church-beginnings went back to the ninth century
(and that would be a thousand years ago) and that there was
a branch of the church that was called *Calixines* that had
something to do with a Greek word, she thought, for cup,
like calix is a word for part of a flower that is like a cup.

There were flowers that were like flat daisies or roses,
she said, on the old belt, and Ida said they were called water
lilies, water roses in German, so maybe the lily I held in my
hand and afterwards put on Papalie's grave (straight up, stuck
in the ground so that it looked as if it were growing there)
could be a rose, too. Maybe the white rose and the black rose
that Mamalie used to talk about to Aunt Laura and Mama
(when they got too excited and laughed too much about
nothing at all) are the shadow of the *Calixines* rose that I
had given me by the man who I thought was the gardener,
who drove the sleigh. Maybe, when Mamalie looks up and
says, "Thank you, Hilda, isn't it time you were in bed?" I
will see that it was all a sort of dream that I made it up, that
Mamalie never did say anything about an Indian who was
at *Wunden Eiland,* who was named Shooting Star.

Maybe, it was just that I was dreaming something be-
cause I was afraid a shooting star might swish out of the sky
and fall on the house and burn us all up. Maybe, it was be-
cause I was afraid of being burnt up that I made Mamalie, in

the dream, say she wasn't just afraid of being burnt up—though she was afraid—only she was more afraid that she might lose the papers. The papers were lost.

"Here is your glass of water, Mamalie," I say.

But though I call her Mamalie, so that she can now be herself out-of-a-dream, she says, "Thank you, thank you, Lucy." She says, "Yes, Lucy, you're right. . . .

"What was it young Brother Francis was saying yesterday? Yesterday, he said that nothing is lost; there are things, he says (like the invisible plant forms in the drops of water he studies under his new microscope), in the human soul that have not yet been discovered.

"It was cool in the room and when he finished the communion prayer for the sick, I felt that I wasn't burning up anymore. Don't mind, Lucy. It was the fever. I was burning up with fever. Yes, Lucy, tell Brother Francis if he calls for vespers, that I'm all right. Tell Brother Francis when he comes for vespers."

She says "vespers" and the word "vespers" means those meetings they have sometimes, almost like love feasts, when they have coffee and sugar cake around a table.

It is sitting round a table and talking about the sand island and *Christiansbrunn* and the *Singstunden* and *Liturgien* and the famous water music on the river in the old days, and the tree here or the tree there that was cut down, what a pity! And remembering the time when the steel mills had not even been thought of, and now Bother Francis is taking her hand and saying that he will not speak again of these things that have troubled her unless she herself particularly wants it, and that he will tell no one of it; it must have happened, he said, he could not doubt her word nor question the reality of the experience and Henry Seidel's concern about the matter, though poor Brother Henry had been overworking for a long time and had burnt himself up with zeal and devotion.

There had been strange forces at work, he said, in this great land from the beginning, and the Indian ritual in the early days was not understood, and after all, it was not so very many years since the massacre at *Gnadenhuetten*.

(*Gnadenhuetten*? So they had been killed at *Gnadenhuetten*.)

I cannot follow what Elizabeth Caroline and Brother Francis are saying; I cannot hear what they are saying, but I have a feeling that our own grandfather had heard stories—from his grandfather even—that brought fear and the terror of burning and poisonous darts (that *arrow that flieth by day*) very near.

It was not just a thing that had happened even in the days of Papalie's grandfather, it was something that might still happen.

I seem to hear Brother Francis talking it out with Mamalie, very clearly and in the most understanding and sympathetic way, recalling the early missions and the work of Zeisberger and the young Count, Christian Renatus, yet seeing the other side, seeing the extravagances, the plays and processions and the strange gatherings, as a sort of parody on their saviour and the story of the gospel, which shone clear and in simple symbols for him.

The redeemer was not to be parodied (however sincere the feeling back of it) in robes and processions through the streets of this very town. Our saviour was not to be worshipped in a startling transparency which showed the wounds, wide and red and blood dripping, when a candle was pushed forward, back of the frame, in the dark.

There were actual extravagances too, practical issues,

the question of church funds squandered in these elaborate meetings that were ritualistic sort of parties, really, where certain favorites of the group bore the names of the followers of our Lord.

These things, remembered, heard about, forgotten, passed through Papalie's mind; he did not want to offend dear Sister Elizabeth Caroline, who had so recently lost her husband. He would wait. But he feared that she had been carried away by some feverish phantasy; he has loved and admired his colleague, Henry Seidel, and their families had been bound up in the interests of the Moravian Brotherhood for generations. He thought of Henry's little daughter.

"I will look in on little Agnes, on the way home," he said. "I met Sister Maria Bloom actually, coming here," he said. "Rest," he said, "I will look after your little Agnes."

I seem to hear him say "little Agnes," or is it Mamalie who says "Agnes?" Mamalie says "Agnes," so whoever I am, I am not now Lucy.

I was Lucy or old Aunt Lucia when I went over to the washstand, when I thought, "If she looks up and says, 'Why aren't you in bed, Helen' or 'What are you doing here in my room at this hour, Hilda,'" then I will know that all that about Shooting Star was a dream or a sort of waking dream or just thoughts while I was sitting there in her bed, picking out the patches of the old dresses they wore and the *pervanche* blue, she called it, that one of the old-girls from New Orleans sent Mamalie in a letter once, to show her the color of her bridesmaid's dress when her sister was married.

That was that other patch, very blue but not very bright blue, like some of the pansy petals when they are two colors of blue. We didn't talk about that patch, but I can say I was thinking of asking her about that patch—it's not a very large patch—if she asks me what I was thinking, or even what I was saying.

Really, I am Agnes now, so I suppose I ought to call her Mimmie again. "Here is your water," I say, "Mimmie."

"I remembered that *the leaves were for the healing of the nations* and I drank the water in the goblet . . . what was I saying, what was I saying, Hilda?"

I said, "You were saying you were thirsty, Mamalie, and I got you some water from the pitcher on the washstand, it isn't very cold; I was thinking, would you want me to run down and get some cracked ice? I could run down and get some cracked ice from the refrigerator. You were saying . . ."

Mamalie, Mamalie, Mamalie, what were you saying? Wait, Mamalie, there are a thousand questions that I want to ask you.

Mamalie, Mamalie, you have told me nothing at all, really did they ever find the papers that were lost? Mamalie, this is all frightful, I could cry with sorrow and grief that you won't tell me more, because now you are holding the common kitchen tumbler in your hand, and it's only a kitchen tumbler. I remember Mama saying, before you came, "We really must look out an odd glass or a pretty cup for the washstand in the spare bedroom, before your grandmother comes."

Why, Mamalie, I could die of grief when I think we had just such a common kitchen tumbler instead of a crystal goblet, and Mamalie, don't you want the cracked ice; it's really only water from the washstand pitcher, and I could have run down and got some cracked ice, but you understand, I was so excited, I couldn't wait a minute, I wanted to hear more about *Wunden Eiland* and *Gnadenhuetten* and they were killed—they were killed, the little huts of the blessed in the habitation of Grace are burning, and the leaves on the young dogwood trees are withered, and Paxnous is far away because he was trying to keep the tribes from fighting.

Oh, Mamalie, there is such a lot I want to know; I want to know what Paxnous' wife looked like, she was a sort of Princess and Oh, there is Anna von Pahlen, my dear, dear Anna who was Morning Star like the Princess with the nine brothers in the story that was lost, and she had lilies too, like I had a lily, only it was a short stem like a white cup, like a goblet, not like the branch of lilies the Madonna has on Easter cards or Jesus has on Easter cards when He comes out of the tomb, *passe le tombeau*.

Mamalie, Mamalie, don't go away, Mamalie; I told you I'd get you some cracked ice because you were burning with a terrible sort of fever, which was when you remembered how you were burnt; but you weren't burnt at *Gnadenhuetten* when the Indiana massacred the Inhabitants of Grace, but it was the other Indians who did it; Oh Mamalie, say it wasn't Paxnous who gave his wife, the Princess Morning Star, to the Moravians.

Mamalie, don't go away. Because the thing that will happen, will happen to me this winter after Christmas or before Christmas begins, about November, but I won't remember. I will forget, like you forgot all about *Wunden Eiland* and the papers that were lost and I will be afraid too. Mamalie, there will be savages, and they will have ugly symbols like some of the bad Indians, to bring ugly and horrible things back to the world and the *Storm of Death* is storming in my ears now; Mamalie wait, there is so much I want to ask you.

Mamalie, Mamalie, you say you don't want any cracked ice, though I could run down to the refrigerator and get you some cracked ice that Ida always has, in a bowl for ice water in the refrigerator. Mamalie, you said *rivers of crystal* and that is like the ice storms that we have, when the trees glisten like glass in a fairy tale of a glass mountain, and there is always the moment in the woods when you remember a path (that you couldn't remember) that will run to an old ford across a stream or a river, that will run to a spring that is called *Christiansbrunn* because it was Christian Renatus who helped find out the secret, though hardly anyone knows now that there even was a secret.

Mamalie, you are holding the glass of water, and you are looking at the glass of water, and you saw a picture in the crystal goblet, that was Papalie and Aunt Lucia who were standing at a window, and I think there was a white curtain blowing in the wind, but you didn't tell me. Mamalie, don't get lost; I must go on, I must go on into the darkness that was my own darkness and the face that was my own terrible inheritance, but it was Papa, it was my own Papa's face, it wasn't the face of the wounded one at *Wunden Eiland,* though I got them all mixed up, but I will get them separated again and I will hold the cup in my hand that is a lily, that is a rose, that is . . .

✳ *WHAT IT WAS*

What it was, was not appreciable at the moment. What happened did not take long to happen.

We were sitting round the round table in the sitting room; there was a painting book and a glass for paint water and Ida had gone upstairs and the baby was asleep and Eric and Mr. Evans were at the observatory or the transit house, or in their rooms in the wing of the house.

Mama and Papa had gone to Philadelphia, the way they did if it was raining or if there were clouds so Papa could not work. Papa would leave the party, or what they called a reception, if he thought it was going to clear up, and Mama would have to come home alone afterwards, if she wanted to stay on after he left.

We did not ourselves go in to Philadelphia very often; it was a long trip with a sort of streetcar with an engine that ran the two miles to Cobbs Creek that was the city limit and then another half-hour in the ordinary trolley, to Wanamaker's to see the Christmas things or to go with Mama to see Cousin Laura and Cousin Emily Bell on Spruce Street. This was our house. We had moved here after Christmas, one winter.

I had come first, alone with Papa and Mama, and we had stayed at Fetters' Farm, which was the nearest house except the farmhouse and the cowsheds which belonged to the Flower Farm. An old man had left his farm to the university for an observatory and this was it; it was Flower Observatory and Papa was the astronomer and Eric and Mr. Evans helped him with his work.

We had a big Thanksgiving dinner, and the uncles and the aunts came, and Mama gave an Easter party, like we always had, and the university ladies helped hunt the eggs with their children that they brought. Mama drew bunnies in ink on top of the invitation, or a nest with a duck or a chick with its eggshell, and some of the letters they wrote back to say they were coming had ducks or bunnies drawn on, too.

Everybody liked the little baskets Mama bought, and Harold and I helped with the smaller children, but it was a long way to Philadelphia and we did not have little parties, only sometimes one big party like that, or when they all came, Thanksgiving Day. People did not run in and Mama did not run out across the garden to Mamalie or up Church Street to Aunt Jennie's, and Uncle Fred did not go past the house and wave his music at us (when we shouted at him to come in) and say, "I'm late for choir practice."

Eric took us for walks. There was not the river and the boats and the summerhouse on the island. Dr. Snively lived two miles down the road and the Snivelys came sometimes with their pony to take us out; they were de Forest and Margaret and Ethelwyn and Muriel. They lent me their books and I lent them mine. They had a *Red Fairy Book* and there were some of my old stories in it, but with different pictures. The mailman did not pass the house, but we had to go for the mail to Upper Darby which was a little town, Mama said, a village. It was just below the school where we went. We did not like the school, but we never said anything about it. Maybe, Gilbert did like it; he played baseball with the older boys. Sometimes Harold and I went off on the path in the woods, but they would not let us go beyond the first fence through the woods, because there were gypsies camping there sometimes. It was the Sellers' woods. The Sellers had a big old house that we went to sometimes. The Sellers were Quakers or Friends, they called them. The best house was the Ashursts, that was about two miles away or nearer, if you went across the fields, or maybe it wasn't much more than a mile. The Ashursts only lived there in the summer, the house was called the *Grange* because that was what they said the Marquis de Lafayette had called it or they named it for his house; anyhow he and George Washington had walked along a road through the woods that they called Lafayette's Walk. There were box hedges and a big round bed of heliotrope in the summer in front of the house.

It was quiet in the room and Gilbert was cutting out some paper soldiers with Papa's shears that he wasn't supposed to take from Papa's table, unless he put them back before Papa got home. Harold was helping me with the paintbook that was almost all painted in, and the piano was there, like it was in the old house with Mama's books of music piled on top; she played *Traumerei* when I asked her, but she did not play the piano so much. She said I must have music lessons, but it was too far to go to Philadelphia. Doctor Snively said I could come to their house and have a lesson when Margaret and Ethelwyn and Muriel had their lessons, twice a week on Tuesday and Friday. Mama said it would be too much to ask, and Doctor Snively said the children were so happy to have neighbors at last; de Forest was Gilbert's age or a little older and Margaret was a little older than I. I was between Margaret and Ethelwyn. Soon, I would begin these music lessons, Mama said. The piano was open and there was the Venus that Mama had brought back from Europe, from Paris. The Venus was called *Venus de*

Milo and there were the same pictures we had in the old house, and some more of the photographs of places they had been to in Europe, on the stairs.

The old streetcar or steamcar went past the house once an hour; it was going past soon; we knew when the times were, ten minutes past the hour when it was on time. There was a switch opposite the Fetters' farm, where the two cars passed each other, the one going to the city and the other coming back, and sometimes they were late. We would wait for the steamcar that ran with a sort of engine, not fastened to the car but part of it. The steamcar went past the house and we waited because perhaps they would come back, but they did not come back, so we went on.

Gilbert went out in the hall, then he came back. Then he took the shears and put them on Papa's table. "But he hasn't come back," I said. Harold was painting a yellow ruffle on a dog that looked like the dog in our old *Punch and Judy*; the dog, in the colored picture that we were meant to copy the uncolored picture from, had a red ruffle. I did not know if Harold was making it different on purpose; you can hardly see the yellow in the lamplight.

"The yellow will look different in the morning, yellow looks different at night," I told Harold. I did not say, "But you should have painted the ruffle red," because we did not always paint the picture the same as the colored picture on the opposite page.

I said, "Yellow looks different in the morning." Harold said, "I know." The clock was ticking very loudly. Annie should come in and tell us to go to bed, but when Papa and Mama were out they did not always tell us. Now it would be another hour for the trolley to pass the house. We had a driveway past the house; it would be better, Mama told Doctor Snively or the Ashursts when they drove up and their wheels scrunched the pebbles, in the spring, "The university is having it properly tarred and rolled," Mama said. There were three big maple trees and a wild cherry tree by the road, but they said it was not any good for fruit, and in the wrong place, anyway, and it would have to be cut down; there were little trees planted back of the kitchen, they were peach trees, but we had not had any peaches yet. The Ashursts sent things from their garden, iris roots and different shrubs for the shrubbery.

Well, now there was only the next car to wait for, or Ida or Annie to come in and tell us to go to bed; Gilbert was waiting, his elbows were on the table, he was pretending not to look at us, but he was looking at us. This was the same table that we had in the old house, in the sitting room there. We put on a white cloth and flowers and presents on this table for birthdays, but there would be no birthday for a long time; all of our birthdays came near together, mine in September, the two boys' in October. Harold went on painting.

There was a bump on the front porch by the steps, as if someone were coming up, "Perhaps it's them," I said, but then it was quiet. Gilbert started putting his new cut-out paper soldier in the shoe box where he had the other old ones. Then I thought I heard someone bump again and I ran out to the front door. I opened the front door. The light from the lamp in the hall showed the porch, it was empty, there were two benches built in the wall that made a little open room of the roofed-in part of the porch by the door.

It was dark and I could not see; the bright light from the hall went over the floor of the porch only as far as the steps, then the dark. I stood and looked at the dark beyond the porch steps and then Papa walked across the light.

He walked right across the floor and I said, "Oh, Papa," and ran out, with the door wide open. I took his hand and I said, "Oh, Papa," and he didn't say anything. He did not hold my hand tight in his hand, he did not take my hand the way he usually did, his fingers did not close tight round my hand the way they always did. It had never happened before that his fingers did not close round my hand.

His hand did not seem to belong to him, his arm seemed like the arm of a scarecrow or a rag doll. I pulled at his sleeve, and his sleeve and his arm did not seem to pull him. I pulled at the overcoat he had on, I pulled at his coat, he was swaying back and forth. Was this a drunk man? Is this how drunk people act, and he had no hat on, and now I pulled him to the open door and I looked at him . . . and I looked at him.

I pulled him in the door, he stood on the rug on the hall floor. There was the rug on the floor and I did not see anything except Papa's face, but I knew what was in the hall, but it went far away, then it came clear, then everything in the hall was peculiar; I mean it had some special place and some special reason for being there, as if it were things you cut out of the back of magazines and paste in your paper-doll house. That is not just what I mean, but that is what I mean.

The clock stood there and ticked and it was a clock that belonged to a story, it was a clock that had a door that went into a tunnel, that led to a house in the woods, and the old man and the old lady on the mantelpiece in the hall (that they had brought back with the square dish with the tulip and the rose painted on it, from Dresden) were like an old man and an old lady in a fairy story who come alive after the clock strikes midnight.

The clock would not strike for a little while, the car ran past the house at ten minutes past the hour and the car was late and then we had waited a little, so the clock would not strike the hour for perhaps half an hour or almost three-quarters of an hour. The hour was cut in half, it might be almost the half-hour, because Gilbert had said when he came back from putting Papa's desk shears back on his table, "The old car's late, as usual."

He had said that, I remembered it now. Harold was sitting at the table and I said, "Yellow looks different by daylight," and he said, "I know." Harold was sitting at the table and Gilbert was putting his new cut-out soldiers in the shoe box. But really we were in the hall.

Gilbert shut the front door. Harold was there by me and I pulled at Papa's coat. I pulled at his coat and I pulled him in to his study and Gilbert got the lamp from the hall. When he was pushed down in the chair by his table, my face was almost as tall as his head when he was sitting down, so it looked nearer.

The blood was running down from the side of his face that was by me, and there was dust on his coat, and the arm that I had pulled at on the porch hung over the chair.

His eyes were wide open but he did not seem to know us. He sat in his chair. There was the lamp on the table that Gilbert must have put there and Gilbert was not there. Harold and I were alone with him and he did not seem to know us and he did not shut his eyes and his eyes went on looking and looking.

I ran into the kitchen with Harold and we filled the washbasin with water and brought back a towel and Harold stood there and now the water in the basin was almost as red as the blood on his face and his beard was thick with blood and I went on washing his face with the towel and wringing out the towel in water, like Ida showed me how to do when I was a little girl and helped her and Annie wash clothes, but that was in the old house.

This was the new house and we thought, "What fun it will be to move and go to a new house," and now we were here and we had little peach trees in the back garden by the kitchen porch and we had new plants and roots for the shrubbery that the Ashursts sent us. Where was Mama? Was Mama outside, was she dead?

Where was everybody? I went on wringing out the towel and the basin got more red and it did not really seem to matter. Nothing mattered because everything was somewhere else. Gilbert was cutting out paper soldiers and I was watching Harold paint the dog ruffle yellow and we were sitting at the round table in the sitting room and we were waiting for the car that came, if it was on time, ten minutes past the hour, but it was late as usual, Gilbert said.

Where is Gilbert? I must go and empty this basin and get some more fresh water. I must get another towel. But I cannot leave him alone and we are alone in his room. This is his study. There is the desk, there are his ink bottles and his pens and the shears that Gilbert took and that Gilbert put back, and I said, "But he hasn't come in yet."

He hadn't come in but he had been somewhere near and something had happened, while the car went on past the house. Was it robbers? Something had happened that only happens in stories. *The Arabian Nights* had a picture of a lady whose head might be cut off but it wasn't, because she went on telling a man in a turban, who was a Turk (or did they say he was Arabian?), a new story. This was a picture in that book or it was the Bible picture when we spread the illustrated Bible open on the floor, before we could read the writing. He was on the stairs, too. On the stairs, He was looking and looking and never shutting his eyes and the thorns made great drops of blood run down his face and Mama thought it was a beautiful Guido Reni.

Harold was there, he held the basin. I could not get the thick blood out of my father's beard. It tore like my doll's hair, when it gets tangled. If the water was hot, maybe we could get the thick blood out of his beard. I wanted hot water and I wanted a new towel, but if we went out for some more water, then he would be alone. You cannot leave him alone, staring.

He looks at the bookcase where he has his *War and Peace* and Victor Hugo's *Les Misérables* and some German books in German. Those are his reading books (his other books are all along the wall, the other side of the table) and his Gibbon's *Rome*. I have tried to read in these books because they have covers striped like marbles, with dark blue on the back and triangles of dark blue on the corners; he said I could read them, but I did not read very far in Gibbon's *Rome*.

He is looking at the glass doors of the bookshelf, it is part of an old desk, there is a drawer in the desk that opens; in it, he keeps his pistol. "Did you ever shoot a man?" He said he never did that he knew of, but now someone or something had shot him or hit him, like an Indian with a tomahawk. You could see that something had hit him. If he goes on looking at the glass door of the shelves, above the old desk, where he keeps his pistol in the drawer, I will have to push his head round, I can't have him go on looking at one thing like that. If he would close his eyes, it would be better, it would even be better if he fell down but we would not be able to get him up; do dead men sit in chairs?

He walked across the bright light from the open door and I said, "Papa," and he didn't say anything. What he says, when I say "Papa," is "little one" or he says *"Töchterlein,"* and when I take his hand, his hand shuts round my hand like it does, and he holds my hand almost too tight sometimes and he even calls me daughter.

Then Ida was there, she said, "What?" I saw her stand in the door, she said "How? Where?" She went away. She had her hair up, she pins it round her head, she takes it down in front of the little mirror in her room and makes two long plaits of it, but she hadn't taken it down; I might have thought she was in bed, but I had not really thought about her; now she was there. She went away. The door to the wing opened and Eric and Mr. Evans were there; now I saw why Gilbert had gone away, he had gone to get Eric and Mr. Evans. Ida came back, she had more towels, she pushed me away, she said, "Run away, run away," what did she mean? She had a bowl, it was one of the big china bowls, there are a lot of them and they all fit in together; she had water in the bowl but we had done all that; Harold still held the basin. She said, "Put it down, I'll see to your father," as if he were coming in for his evening coffee, or something; she pushed in front, I could not see Papa. Eric and Mr. Evans stood there in the way.

Now I stood there trying to get round to Papa, but they said, "It's all right."

Mr. Evans said, "You children run along"; where were we to run to? Now Mama was standing in the doorway. There was Papa in the chair, Ida, Eric and Mr. Evans and Gilbert and Harold and me, and Mama in the doorway. She said, "Charles." That is all she said.

She had on a lace scarf or a lace shawl over her head, like she wears when she doesn't wear a hat, when she goes out at night. It was black lace over her head like the lady on the inside lid of the cigar box that Papa gave me. He saved two boxes and gave them together; mine had the lady with the shawl like Mama had and Gilbert had a man in a big hat with a bullfight on the little pictures round the edge, on the inside of his tobacco box.

They were cigar boxes, there was writing in Spanish, he said it was from Cuba.

Now he saved the two boxes and gave Gilbert the one with the man and me the one with the lady. Maybe Harold was too small for a box. I never, till now, wondered what Harold had, but maybe he was too small. This was in the old house, we cut out pictures for valentines and kept them in the boxes, then we kept firecrackers in the boxes. He always gave us his boxes. Now I must have remembered the box because of the lady with the lace over her head, and the little pictures were of red and white flowers and there was a gold edge around the whole picture on the inside lid, like a valentine. It was like that.

He smoked a cigar after dinner sometimes, or when professors came to talk, but he liked his pipe. The bowl with the tobacco was on the top of the chest of drawers that ran along the wall next to his table. He had them made for his study, before we came here. He let us look over the blueprints with the architect, who came from Philadelphia with the blueprints for the new house, and he would take his pen and make a little mark here, a door here or a cupboard under the stairs. This was that house.

We had watched him draw a square for the extra door in the hall that led out to the field that was now the orchard, since the peach trees were planted. We had seen the blueprint for this room, the double window that looked out on the orchard, the bookshelves built in for his books and nautical almanacs that were on the other side of the table; there was the sofa where he lay down in the afternoons, sometimes when he had been working at night. There was the door where Mama was standing with the lace over her head, there was the wing door that had opened a crack when Gilbert slid in first, that had opened wide when Mr. Evans and Eric walked in.

Gilbert must have run down the wing stairs to get there first. That is what he had gone away for (perhaps even to the observatory or the transit house), he had not really left us alone, but Harold and me were alone for a long time.

Now they did not say, "Where did you find your father?" They did not ask, "Who found him?" They did not say, "But this is your father, were you alone with your father? Did you wash his face? Who got the basin? Who held the basin? Who washed his face?" They did not say any of this, because now Ida had spread a towel over his coat, as if it was the barber's, and was pressing round his head with her hands.

No one said, "But who found him?" They said, "Run along, run along." Mama did not look at us, she was looking at Papa. She did not say, "Oh, children, children, who was it found your father?"

What we did was, we sat on the sofa in the sitting room. There was the paint glass on the table and the paintbrush where Harold had dropped it when we ran out, and there was the shoebox with Gilbert's soldiers. Now I heard the clock tick. I had not heard it for a long time, but it must even have struck because Mama was back and the car only ran once an hour. I did not hear the clock strike. It was long after our bedtime. Gilbert sat at the top of the sofa and I was next and then Harold. We did not say anything to each other.

Eric and Mr. Evans came in, they talked about "concussion" and they wondered how soon the doctor could possibly get here. Who had gone for the doctor? You would think it would be Eric or Mr. Evans; maybe they got Annie to go for the doctor. Where would the baby sleep tonight? What was "concussion"? Had he been out there a long time, had he maybe been on the streetcar before this one? Had it happened an hour before? Or had it just happened when it did? Had he fallen off the car? Had someone tried to kill him? Was he dead? How would they get him upstairs? What was Mama doing? What is concussion? Someone must ask but I did not know if it would be me or Gilbert.

"Yes, yes, yes," said Eric, very fast, all in one word, and as if he were answering himself, "yes, yes," very quiet. He stood there and Mr. Evans said, "Concussion of the brain and his collarbone is broken."

Why did they stand here talking? Why didn't they do something? Or had Annie been sent for the doctor? What was Mama doing alone with him, had they taken him upstairs, how would they get him upstairs?

"Yes, yes, yes," said Eric over and over, and he felt for a cigarette packet in his pocket and he pulled it out and threw it on the table. The little bent green cardboard cigarette packet lay on the table. It was lying on the picture of the dog with the red collar. Someone must say something. Gilbert got up and picked up the packet; he said, "There's a cigarette left, Eric, you threw away a cigarette." Eric said, "Yes, yes," and took the cigarette and did not light it.

Gilbert had got the cigarette packet and he had said, "Eric, you threw away a cigarette," and Harold would not be expected to say anything, so I must say, "What is concussion?"

Gilbert was sitting there again and I said, "What is concussion?"

I heard my words and the way I said the word which I had never heard before and now we would know. It would be something that made him stare at the glass door of the bookshelf and not say anything. It was something to do with his head, "Concussion of the brain," Mr. Evans had said. Maybe, it meant that he would be crazy and never speak any more, or maybe it meant that he would die.

Mr. Evans turned round as if he had not seen us. "What are you waiting for?" Mr. Evans said.

What did he think we were waiting for?

"Isn't it time you went to bed?" Mr. Evans said. We were there in a row, and Eric was twirling the cigarette round in his fingers, then he dropped the cigarette. I waited for Gilbert to pick it up but he did not.

"Ah-er-er—" said Eric, that way he talks, "it's not—it's not—" He did not say, "It's not dangerous," he did not say, "It isn't anything," because he did not tell lies. He did not tell lies to us, he bought us *Puck* and *Judge* which are funny-papers and Mama would say, "You must not spend all your salary the first of the month on the children, you need some new socks," but he went on buying us *Puck* and *Judge* and a bound volume of *Saint Nicholas* though it wasn't Christmas or anybody's birthday.

He bought me a big *Little Women* that had more in it about how they grew up and he took us for long walks and we found a violet-farm near Overbrook. The people there were French and they let us pick all the violets we wanted, though we couldn't talk to them. We tried to understand and they tried to understand and they said, *"pere?"* to Eric and Eric told us he did know that that was French for father and he said, "No, no," which we found was the same in French.

They asked us to have coffee in their little house and they had flat wooden trays for the violets. Then Mama said we must get some more violets and she was very happy and she gave us a dollar to buy them next time; it was too far for her to walk, but she kept telling the university ladies that called, "Think of it, it's several miles, you can see the glass frames from the front porch when the sun is shining on them, and the children came on it quite by accident—it's a violet-farm, they have double Parma violets, the children bought me almost a dozen different kinds of single and double violets, they can hardly talk any English but they got the children to understand they could come back and pick violets to take away."

Those were the sort of big bunches that are very expensive in florists' windows on Walnut and on Chestnut Street in the city and they sell them in tight bunches on the street, with silver paper round the stems and wires, but Mama said "Look they're all loose, such long stems, I really never saw such lovely violets."

It was like that, and she said violets were her favorite flower but roses were hers too, because June sixth was her birthday.

I had thought of birthdays and that they were a long way off and so they were, but Mama's birthday was in June and so would come sooner than ours. The baby's birthday was the second of May, but I was thinking of Gilbert and Harold and me when I thought of how we always had a white cloth on the round table where the paintbox was, and spread the presents on it.

Mama's table was easy because we covered her presents with roses.

Eric said, "We don't know exactly, I mean concussion of the brain is—is if someone gets hit very hard or—er—falls down, then when the head is struck very hard—." I wanted to know exactly what it was and I could see that Gilbert's shoe was kicking at the edge of the rug that wasn't lying quite flat on the floor. If we wanted to get the rug flat, we would have to get off the sofa and lift the sofa, so the little wheel that was fastened in the sofa leg to push it around with would go straight on the rug. We could not get off the sofa, we could not move.

We were frozen stiff to the sofa, in a row, but Gilbert was showing that he could move, if he wanted, by scuffing with his heel at the rug, where it bumped a little, where it had not been pushed quite flat when Ida or Annie had moved the sofa in the morning when they did the sweeping. It was easier, anyhow, for Gilbert to scuff at the floor because his legs were two years' longer. Harold's feet were straight out and he was sitting straight up, as if he were having his picture taken.

I could not scuff at the carpet though my feet reached the carpet, but I pushed myself back so that maybe Harold would feel that I wasn't really waiting so hard, and then maybe Harold would sit back.

"It's like that," said Eric, "if a man falls down—"

"Did he fall down, then?" I was the one that was doing the talking. Gilbert was too busy fastening the leather pad over the knee of his black stocking, that didn't need fastening.

"We—we—don't know—"

Then the clock sort of hammered like a hammer with nails, and Mr. Evans said, "Probably your father slipped, as he was getting off the car, or the car may have backed unexpectedly—there should have been a lamppost set up at the gate, in the beginning. It's quite obvious that your father slipped, that his foot slipped."

Papa wasn't like that. He wasn't the sort of person whose foot slipped.

Mr. Evans walked to the window, then he walked back. Gilbert slid off the sofa.

Mr. Evans said, "I'll take the lantern and go out and see if—" he stopped and Gilbert said, "I'll come with you. He lost his hat."

Mr. Evans said, "No, you wait with the children. I'm

only going out to see if I can find any traces—I mean, do you know, Eric, if his wallet and his watch were taken?"

"I didn't look," said Eric.

"His wallet is in the inside of his coat, or sometimes his overcoat," Gilbert said, "and his watch is in the little watch-pocket."

Mr. Evans said, "Did you see them there?" How could Gilbert have seen them?

"No, no," said Mr. Evans, "you stay here," because Gilbert went to the door and was out in the hall, but he came back.

"They put his overcoat on the bench in the hall," Gilbert said, and Mr. Evans went out and Mr. Evans came back with Papa's black wallet and he laid it on the top of the piano and he said, "That's all right."

He was thinking, and we knew he was thinking, "Then well, it wasn't robbers," but did that make it any better? It would be almost better to think it was robbers, that they had hit Papa for something, that there was some kind of a reason for it, not just this waiting and wondering what concussion was. Mr. Evans went into the hall again, then he opened the front door, then we heard his feet go down the porch steps.

His feet went down the steps, the lantern was in the hall of the wing. He could go to the hall in the wing by walking through Papa's study that had that door that opened into the wing.

He did not go through Papa's study. He had gone down the porch steps. Then he would turn round the rockery, in the corner between the porch and the path to the wing that led off the drive. If we listened, we might hear when he opened the wing door, but we did not hear.

Gilbert walked round as if nothing were happening and then he took off the lid of the shoebox that his paper soldiers were piled up in. He just took off the lid and shook the box, the way he does to get the paper soldiers in flatter, and he pressed them down with his hands, like he does to make them not take up so much room, and I got up and walked a little.

We were going to walk around the room and we were going to take a book out of the bookshelf, that Papa had made. The bookshelf was on the wall over the sofa. Papa had his workbench and his saw and hammer and tools in the cellar now; "But it's a perfect workroom," the ladies from the university said when they were being shown around the house, "and so warm with that huge furnace." There were high little windows in the cellar and it was like a big room with the windows small and high up. The floor was cement, Eric said the floor was cement. It was hard, but the cellar was not dark like the cellar in the old house and there were the rakes and the hoe there, and we had the same big box with the lid, with our shoe-blacking things in it.

Papa made the shelf over the sofa, it was varnished too. It was William Morris furniture, Mrs. Schelling said, whatever that was, and he made me a bench for my room like that, and he made a wooden table for the porch.

We were going to walk around the room. Gilbert had begun it, and we were going to do things like we always did, so I said, "Harold, you dropped your paintbrush on the floor, did you know?" And Harold slid off the sofa and picked up his paintbrush and he picked up Eric's cigarette.

He stood looking at the cigarette, as if he did not know what to do next, but Gilbert had picked up the shoebox and was shaking it to get the paper soldiers to take up less room, because the lid bulged when it was on and would fall off if he did not tie it up with string or get a big elastic band from Papa's table. He would go and ask Papa for a big rubber band for his box of paper soldiers, everything would be just like that, but Harold would have to say something or do something, because just to stand there was not doing what we were doing.

I mean, we were doing a charade or a game we called dumb-crambo, when you act words. But Harold would have to be pushed like you do Laddie and Georgine when they make us have them in our games. Only Harold is older and Harold is not a dumb child, though Mama still says she is worried because he talks so little. But why should Harold talk?

"What's that?" I said to Harold as if I did not know. "Oh, it's that cigarette," I said, "Oh Eric, it's that cigarette you lost. We found the cigarette you lost."

Now Eric would come in too and we would play this charade like we did in this room, with the audience sitting in the other room that was the parlor, or people called the parlor a reception room now. The double doors could be shut, so when we played charades we shut the double doors and worked out the word, then we opened them.

Then we left them open where the Rosa Bonheur *Horse Fair* was on an easel and the picture Mama painted of *Willow Eddy*—that was a place on the old river, where she used to go with trips with Cousin Ed and Cousin Ruth and where she once went to see a gypsy fortune-teller.

That was a long time ago and that was before Mama married Papa.

Eric took the cigarette.

Then Eric looked at the cigarette.

I often wondered what the fortune-teller told Mama, all of it I mean; Mama said the fortune-teller said, she would have a child who would have a gift, but Mama always said to the university ladies when they talked about Uncle Fred and the Bach Choir at Bethlehem, "It's funny that the children are not gifted."

Now, if Eric were playing a charade, he would light his

cigarette. Now I could not tell everyone what to do, but I waited and he saw I was waiting.

The fortune-teller said Cousin Ruth would not marry Sammy Martens and Cousin Ruth was cross, Mama said, and Sammy Martens went away to Pittsburgh where his uncle was in the steel works there, and Cousin Ruth never married anybody. The fortune-teller, Mama said, had told her she would marry someone; it would be someone with a gift (or there was something about a gift) or it would be a foreign person who was rich but I do not know who that was, and Mama did not tell us about any foreign people she knew who had come to Bethlehem who were rich, and who had gone away; maybe it was someone from the steel mills there, because people were always coming to talk to Uncle Hartley from Pittsburgh.

Eric put his hand in his coat pocket and he found his box of matches. Gilbert got up and got the flat green saucer ash tray, from the mantelpiece.

There are the Boy and the Girl there; in the hall, is the Old Man and the Old Lady; Mama brought the Boy and the Girl back, too, from her honeymoon. The Girl has her skirt tucked up and they both have bare legs and they are fisherboy and fishergirl. The Boy has a net on a stick, like for catching butterflies, over his shoulder, and the Girl has a basket and there are two blue fish-heads poking out of the lid of the basket.

Eric dropped the match in the flat green saucer ash tray, and Gilbert put the ash tray on the table and Gilbert said, "Where's the new copy of *Saint Nicholas*, Hilda, where did you put the new *Saint Nicholas?*"

I was watching Eric to see if his cigarette was really lighted, but it was and he was smoking, and he looked at Harold as if he had just seen him and he looked at Gilbert, then he took a pull on his cigarette and looked around the room, then he said, "Thank you, Harold," then he said, "Thank you, Gilbert, thank you"; he said, "Yes, yes, yes," like he does, all in one word and said, "What are you doing? What are you painting, Hilda?"

I said I wasn't painting, it was Harold, and Harold came and stood by me and Eric turned over the pages of the paint-book.

"Oh," said Eric and he turned back the pages and he said, "Maybe that painting isn't dry yet, I don't want to smudge your painting, Harold."

He pressed the middle of the book flat with his other hand and we were back at the picture of the dog with the collar and the clown with the hoop and the lady who was standing on a horse on one toe and who would jump through the hoop. This was a circus and we had been to a circus; when we first came to Philadelphia, Papa took us to a circus; there was a lady in a cage with lions, dressed like the prince in my old Grimm and she shot off a pistol and she said "hi-hi" and cracked a whip and shot off the pistol again and the lions jumped around the cage but Papa said they couldn't possibly eat her, they were old lions, he guessed and he laughed because we thought the lady would be eaten.

"It's dry," Harold said.

"Yes, yes," said Eric, "Oh yes, I see."

I said, "He did that a long time ago, he did that before—" and then I remembered the bump on the front porch and the way Gilbert had put back the desk shears and the way I was thinking I was glad that Annie had not come in and told us to go to bed.

Gilbert was watching Eric turn over the pages, now Eric turned over to the boys fishing on the bridge and the mill with the boat and he said, "That's a nice boat—I—er—we must take a trip on the river sometime, I mean the Delaware river," he said. "We could take one of those steamboats at the wharves at the end of Market Street, we could take a whole day trip. There is a steamboat, Mr. Evans told me, that runs right down the river to Cape May."

I said, "What is Cape May?" and he said, "Oh, it's the name of a place, it's in New Jersey, it's the seashore."

Gilbert said, "Like Point Pleasant where we went once," and Eric said yes, it was; he hadn't been to Point Pleasant but that is what it was like, there was lots of sand and shells and you could walk for miles along the ocean and there was always a place where you could buy balloons he thought, but he was sure we could get peanuts, he said. He said peanuts grew in New Jersey and they had farms of peach trees and he said things grew in New Jersey like melons because it was so sandy, we would find a place and get a watermelon; he dropped the ash off into the green saucer.

"Let me see," he said. "We can't go yet, we'll go as soon as the excursion boats start; we could even," he said, "take a boat to Baltimore."

I had a girl in Baltimore was a song we sang.

Nellie was a girl that Eric was going to marry, but when we said, when he was shaving in the bathroom in the old house, "How's Nellie, how's Nellie?" and sat on the edge of the bathtub, he said "I wouldn't—" and he turned his face to get the light on the side from the window, where he was shaving.

We waited for him to get off the soap from his chin, and we waited for what he would say, but he didn't say anything so "*I had a girl in Baltimore,* Nellie, Nellie, Nellie," Gilbert went on with it, to the wrong tune, he was just singing anything.

Then Eric turned round with the soap off his face and he was wiping the razor on a towel and he took up another towel and dabbed at his face and we saw blood on the towel.

"You cut yourself," Gilbert said.

Eric said, "Yes, yes, yes," and then he said, "Confound it," which isn't real swearing but Mama said we must not say it. Gilbert kicked his heels on the bathtub, holding on by his hands, we put our tin duck, tin fish, small tin boat that was no bigger than the fish, tin swan, tin frog in that tub. We had the window open and we floated our soap bubbles out of the window till someone wanted to come in, "I told you children you must not lock the door and play games in here," Mama said, so we were not to lock the door.

Eric held his handkerchief to his face now as if he had the toothache; we said "Nellie, Nellie" at him again, and he looked at the handkerchief and did not put it back and there was the cut on his chin, but it was not bleeding very much now, and he said in a different voice, "I would be very glad if you wouldn't—make games about Nellie anymore or—or say Nellie to me anymore."

Then he went and got his coat and went out to wherever it was he was going.

Eric was leafing through the book and he came to the orchard and the cow in the orchard. It was spotted like the pony in the circus picture. It was like that terrible time, that we never told anybody about, when we were going to a farm in the country and it was a big farm with an old lady and a barn and pigs and about six cows and a bull tied up and hens, and the old lady said we could feed the hens.

What it was, was that Papa and Mama were going to the World's Fair, but they said we must have a happy time too; so we talked about it and talked about it and they thought Point Pleasant was too far and it would be better if Ida took us near, where her cousin had a house; there was a big farm, Cousin Clarence wrote, he had a little church near there, Mama said, and he would look after us.

So we went and looked at the farm and the old lady said it would be nice to have children and we would all help her feed the hens.

Then we went back to the station, where Ida's cousin had a little hot brick house near the station rails. And Ida said, "I don't think we want to go to that farm, it's dirty, we don't want to go there. Here is this nice place and Gilbert can play with Fritzie and you and Harold will be so happy. Now this is a nice place, Mrs. Schneider says we can stay here," and it was terrible, and I do not know what happened that we were so hot and the lady was always cross and went and sat with Ida on rocking chairs and always said, "Run away, don't bother me," and Gilbert went off with Fritzie, who would not let us ride his rocking horse, to get frogs and Harold and I were so hot and there was no one to talk to, but Cousin Clarence came and took us to see nice people who let us sit on their porch and they had apple trees.

It was waiting and waiting and every day saying, "Have they sent us a letter?" And the lady who was the mother of Fritzie said, "Maybe your father and mother sent you here to get rid of you, but I don't want you, you needn't think I want you"; I saw her count green dollar bills with Ida. And I thought, that is the money that Papa gave for us to go to the farm and Ida was counting two heaps of the money and they each had a heap and maybe it was true, maybe they had gone to the World's Fair and would never come back, but I was afraid to ask Cousin Clarence because the lady smiled so much and talked with him, and seemed kind and said she was so glad to have us and it was a pity but the farm he had chosen for us was too far away and anyhow old Mrs. Apfelholzer was not anxious to have the children; she said, "She couldn't have them," and that was a lie.

This grown lady told a lie, because the old lady said she wanted us to help her with the hens.

Ida didn't seem like she was and when we were going home at last, she said, "Tell your mother you had a good time, will you," and she gave me a quarter.

I did not know what to do, but when Gilbert started saying he had caught frogs with Fritzie, I didn't say anything. It is a dreadful thing if your mother and father go to the World's Fair and you cannot write a letter and you cannot even read a letter if it comes and even if it comes and you might be able to steal it and take it to Cousin Clarence to read. The lady who was the mother of Fritzie got the letters first and we could only just read our names on the envelope but she kept the letters.

No, I did not really think of all this, when I saw the picture of the apple orchard and the cow, but that funny thing happened that sometimes happens, when there is a hole in the floor or a stone on a walk will open and I will step in and fall down and then I stop running and walk around the stone.

It is something that happens. I never tell anyone about it, for I really do not know what it is about, but it seemed to be there all the time that summer when we were at that hot little brick house, with a horrid flower called a fuchsia that she said "Don't step on" all the time, and none of our toys and books because we were going to a farm where there was a barn and pigs and cows and hens and where we could live like farmer's children and where they said we could get eggs.

Cousin Clarence had written Mama about it and then this lady said old Mrs. Apfelholzer didn't want us and that was a story; it was a grown person who was Ida's cousin, telling a lie.

Cousin Clarence did not know she was telling a lie and

he took Harold and me to a nice place to sit on their porch and they gave us lemonade in blue glasses and they gave us apples and they said, "I wish you were staying here with us," but we had to go back to the hot little house and the lady said, "Well don't eat it then," when I did not like the sausage and pickles and she just took my plate away and she said to Ida, "That will learn her."

So I didn't have any lunch and I didn't tell Cousin Clarence.

Eric turned the pages and he said, "You've almost painted all this book, haven't you?"

He turned the pages back again quickly and bits of the different edges of the pictures were there, and I saw a red slice of paint or a blue, or green of the grass before the big house that looked like the Ashurst's house, where there were bees in the round bed of heliotrope.

The pieces of color did not fit together and seemed to go very fast, like turning that kaleidoscope, it was called, that we took apart and it was little pieces of colored glass and we could not put it together again. It was like that old round box that was at Aunt Millie's house, that Mama had played with when she was a little girl. You put in a strip of long colored pictures, the pictures were like the different pictures of a long funny picture in *Puck* or *Judge,* but they were all in one long piece and were not funny; they were a girl rolling a hoop or a boy jumping a pony over a fence or a lady, like our circus-page in this book, jumping through a hoop in the same kind of clothes, or a man walking with a bear until it stood up on its hind legs.

The colors were separate and bright like the colors in this book, so now when Eric turned over the pages so quickly, it was like lying on the floor with the round box of the gyroscope going round and round. It made you dizzy after a while; you looked through little slats that were just one large slat when the box went fast. Now that was like this.

I held on to the table edge because the box was going so fast and I remembered only a bit of color, the pink and ugly red of the fuchsia flowers that were so ugly and the blue glasses that they gave us and the lemonade, a different color in the glass, and then the old lady, like a good old witch with a broom, who said, "But I always wanted children to hunt my eggs, I need children on this farm," and a picture of an old witch with Hansel and Gretel, because really old Mrs. Apfelholzer (her name was) could not have been a bad old woman in a dirty house like they said, but it was Ida's cousin who was bad and divided the money up with Ida.

I saw the green of the dollar bills as they counted them out like counting cards, for there were three of us and we were to be at that farm while they were at the World's Fair in Chicago, and this was the money for it.

I saw the soap bubble in the tree out of the bathroom window, but that was a whole soap bubble like a balloon made of glass, like the glass mountain the princess climbed, but it was with nails that she climbed up.

I saw the face of the man on the stairs and the way his beard was curly like my doll's hair, and Mama said if Papa cut off his beard she would leave him and everybody laughed; I would not leave Papa if he cut off his beard.

Eric has no beard.

Even the table goes round like the gyroscope on the floor of Aunt Millie's conservatory that isn't a conservatory anymore, but she keeps her old things there and boxes on the shelves where there used to be flowerpots.

Aunt Jennie gave me a Chinese lily that you plant in a bowl with pebbles.

The bowl Aunt Jennie gave me was blue and shiny, the same kind of shine that the green saucer has that Eric puts his ash in.

Eric puts his ash in the saucer, he throws the end of the cigarette down and it smokes beside the matchstick.

The ash curls up and I go on looking at the smoke of the cigarette.

Eric shuts the book.

Gilbert is standing by the piano, looking at Papa's wallet.

The table is round like a big wheel.

There was that man in the milk cart who asked me if I wanted a ride, coming up the Black Horse Hill, home from school, and I said "Yes" and I climbed in.

The horse was pulling at the milk cart, going up the hill, and I was thinking it was fun to have a ride in the milk cart. They drove the carts in, early, to the market on Market Street in Philadelphia, and they came home and slept while the horse climbed Black Horse Hill. The milk cans rattled in the back of a cart, and the horse's back came straight when we came to the top of the hill. There was Fetters' Farm at the top of the hill and the switch where the cars met each other; and the cart jerked and the horse began to run.

I looked at the man and I saw he was . . . he had . . . and he said . . . but I said, "I get out here, I live here," but I did not live at the Fetters' Farm.

I thought he might not stop the horse, so I slid out and I jumped over the wheel that was going fast and I stood by the switch and I saw Mr. Fetters was driving some cows out of their front field and Mrs. Fetters was shelling peas on the porch.

I could pretend to go in at the Fetters' gate, if the man looked to see where I was going, but he did not stop. I saw the back of the cart and the milk tins that rattled and I crept under the fence, so as to get out of the road, and went home through the field, by the side of the road.

The wheel was as big as this table and this table was going round but maybe that was the gyroscope or the soap bubble that I blew out of the window. Once I thought if I had three wishes, like they have in fairy tales, I would wish for a soap bubble to stay as it was with the different rainbows in it and floating over the pear tree, like a balloon, but in my wish it would never break. That was one of my wishes.

Now I do not know what I would wish, except that the table would not go round like that wheel when I jumped and that Eric would take us to a hut in the woods and that we would have *Saint Nicholas* every week instead of only once a month.

Gilbert had asked me where was *Saint Nicholas,* but I did not answer and maybe he was looking for it on the piles of music and magazines on the piano.

Mr. Evans came in; he had Papa's watch in his hand, he said, "I found the Professor's watch and there's someone turning in the drive, I think it's the doctor."

Mr. Evans put down the watch by the wallet that Gilbert had put down again on the piano. Gilbert took up the watch, "It's stopped," he said, "the glass is broken and it's stopped."

Eric took Papa's watch and shook it, Mr. Evans said, "It stopped at quarter past nine, it must have been when—"

There was the crunch of wheels on the drive and Gilbert went to the door.

Mr. Evans said, "But I thought you children were in bed."

The table stopped going round.

"What is concussion, Mr. Evans?" I said.

❊ *MORNING STAR*

"What is concussion, Mr. Evans?" I said. But I could not hear what he said because there was a roar, and then the floor sank.

It was sinking and I was sinking with it, and this was ironical and strange after all we had been through. Now it was ironical and bitter-strange because this was January 17, 1943, and we had done all that. The papers would be burnt, that is what Mamalie had said, she had said the papers would be burnt or she would be burnt, and now it all came back again, now I would be burnt and it did not matter what happened any more, only I did not want to be burnt.

I would sink down and down and all the terrors that I had so carefully held in leash during the great fires and the terrible bombing of London would now break loose, because we hadn't had any big raids for some time and we had forgotten how to act.

We had not quite forgotten, because Bryher had come out of her room and switched off her light and we carefully shut all the doors. I counted the doors. "There are seven doors," I said, although of course we knew this. The hall is narrow, opening from the front door. "I think I'll open the front door," I said, but Bryher said, "No." She sat down on one of the hall chairs and we switched on the small table-lamp and I said, "I think I'll open the front door."

Now I thought, would it be better to dash out through the kitchen to the back door to the fire escape or would it be better to go out of the front door and rush down the five flights of stairs? There is the black-and-fawn-striped carpet in the outer hall and blacked-out windows along the stairs and a muffled blue-shaded light burning on each floor. The lift is useless in a raid, as the electricity may be cut off at any moment, "And there you will be, madame," said the hall porter after one of the big fires, "stuck in the lift and maybe burnt to death and no one could get at you."

The noise was so terrible now that I could not hear what Bryher was saying, but she was saying something. She got up from her chair and took a few steps across the red and grey patterned rug and she stood by my chair. I did not move. The chair would go down too, as if we were both in a lift, an elevator, and we would keep on going down and down. But now the floor was level and I was not going down.

She was not shouting at me but she was speaking carefully. I could see from her face that she was afraid that I was afraid. I *was* afraid. She said it again, and now I heard her words though the noise of little bricks went on; the bricks went on rolling along and knocking against one another and there was now a terrible quiet that was worse than the roar of the guns. "It's nothing," she said, "it's just practice." I knew it was not practice.

I knew the wall outside (not our wall) had fallen. "At first, I thought it was our own wall," I said, "it's because it's so very near. I thought it was our own wall." She said, "No, it's not a wall." She did not shout but her face, like a mask, repeated words. I saw the shape of the words and the way she was keeping her face quiet. Then I heard the words. "It's our new gun," she said.

The bricks were rolling along and now it was quiet but suddenly there was the same terrific roar, and the terrific explosion and the walls shook but the doors did not fly open, pushed outward by the repercussion of the blast as they had done sometimes. So it was not so near or it was nearer; anyhow what she said went with it and I had lost my trick of getting out, of being out of it.

I had learned a trick, lying on my bed, through the closed door, not ten feet away from my right elbow. It had been, I had felt, like a ship; I was snug and comfortable in my bunk, my bed was like a bunk pushed against the wall, in the corner with the outer wall at my head. Then the roar of the wings and the slight trembling of the walls were like the vibration set up in a great ocean liner, and I was on a great ocean liner and the ship might or might not go down. And then there would come that moment when I had left myself lying secure and it did not matter what happened to the frozen image of myself lying on the bed, because there was a stronger image of myself; at least I did not see myself, but I was myself, whether with attributes of pure abstraction or of days and in places that had been the surroundings of my childhood, or whether as sometimes, it seemed, in one of the vast cathedrals of Italy or in a small beehive that was a tiny Byzantine church outside Athens or was actually the beehive tomb of the prehistoric King Agamemnon outside Mycenae, or whether it was a dome of a Mohammedan tomb on the sands of Egypt that rose familiar beyond the gigantic columns of the temples, or whether it was . . . whatever it was, now all the accumulated wealth of being and impression would go down with the ship that was rising and falling.

But it was only my own chair and I never had screamed, I never had fainted, why was Bryher still standing there? She looks at me. Her face is as carved and cold as a Chinese mask, but white, not yellow, not brown or gold. There should be bronze faces and brown and gold faces, there should be the meeting—what was it that Mamalie had tried to tell me?

Now Mamalie was speaking and there was a rattle of the curtain rings as the curtains blew a little inward. It wasn't a thunderstorm, no, it was a star that was going to fall on the house. It was a shooting star that was going to fall on the house and burn us all up and burn us all to death. Bryher is looking at me; she does not know why I am able to sit here. I am sitting here because there is a star, Mamalie told me about it. There was a promise and there was a gift, but the promise it seems was broken and the gift it seems was lost. That is why, now at this minute, there is the roar outside that will, perhaps this time, shatter my head, shatter my brain, and all the little boxes that have been all the rooms I have lived in, have gone in and out of, will fall . . . fall . . . she need not tell me again. Why does she tell me over and over, if it's true, that the sound of the bricks falling is the sound of our own guns?

"It's the sound of our own guns," she says again.

"All right," I say, "it's all right." ·

I saw, I understood . . . a memory of my grandmother's or her grandmother's—a lost parchment, terror that led back finally to the savages, burning and poisonous arrows.

This, I could remember, letting pictures steadily and stealthily flow past and through me. When the terror was at its height, in the other room, I could let images and pictures flow through me, and I could understand Anna von Pahlen who had been the inspirer of the meetings at *Wunden Eiland* when the unbaptized King of the Shawanese gave his beloved and only wife to the Brotherhood; I saw it all clearly.

I remembered how my mind, after a certain pause of

tension and terror, had switched, as it were, into another dimension where everything was clear, where people moved in the costumes of their period, thought back to their old oppressions in Europe and planned a secret powerful community that would bring the ancient secrets of Europe and the ancient secrets of America into a single union of power and spirit, a united brotherhood, a *Unitas Fratrum* of the whole world.

This had not worked out, but it might have worked out and it would work out, I had thought, if I could follow the clue through the labyrinth of associated memories. But I only remembered that I had had this power, the power had gone now; I was a middle-aged woman, shattered by fears of tension and terror, and now I sat in a chair and only remembered that I had been caught up in a vision of power and of peace and I had remembered my grandmother's words exactly.

She had called me Agnes, and she had called me Lucy.

I was Lucy, I was that Lux or Light, but now the light had gone out. There was not even a small candle, although the lamp on the table by my elbow was burning with a soft glow. In the old days, I had kept a bag ready, packed with a few precious possessions, but now I had no shoes on, only a worn pair of bedroom slippers and I had left my handkerchief pushed down between the arm and the padded seat of the chair in the other room, and I couldn't go on this way. I must, if possible, get through this, but I could not go on with it, and I could not achieve the super-human task of bringing back what had been lost, so the Promise might be redeemed and the Gift restored. The Gift was a Gift of Vision, it was the Gift of Wisdom, the Gift of the Holy Spirit, the *Sanctus Spiritus;* actually, it was the same Spirit that Paxnous' people worshipped, with somewhat the same ritual as that of the initiates of *Wunden Eiland.*

I could visualize the very worst terrors, I could see myself caught in the fall of bricks, and I would be pinned down under a great beam, helpless. Many had been. I would be burned to death.

I could think in terms of one girl in a crinoline, I could not visualize civilization other than a Christmas tree that had caught fire.

There had been a little Christmas tree here on the table, where the lamp now was. That was the first tree we had had since the "real" war and the fragile glass balls, I had boasted, had withstood the shock and reverberation of steel and bursting shell; "These little balls," I had said, when I unpacked them from the tangle of tinsel and odds and ends of tissue-paper packing, "are symbolic"; unpicking shredded green tissue paper from a tinsel star, I said, "Look at this, it's as bright as ever and this glass apple isn't broken."

But . . . I was sick to death of tension and tiredness and distress and distorted values and the high-pitched level and the fortitude, which we had proved beyond doubt that we possessed. I had passed the flame, I had had my initiation, I was tired of all that. It had all happened before. Words beating in my brain could get out, not beat there like birds under wire-cage roofs or caught in nets. What was that? The soul? Something being caught or not-caught in the net of the fowler. We were caught. We were trapped. I was sick to death of being on the *qui vive* all the time.

I was tired of trying to understand things, I was tired of trying to explain things. I had done my part. Bryher and my child could go on. I was tired of being the older, the stronger, the more perceptive. I was sick of fanatic courage, my own and that of those about me. We had had too much. The mind, the body is not built to endure so much. We had endured too much. I was tired of it. I could not be brave, I would not be philosophical, it was all a trap, a trick, there could be nothing worse.

I was tired of being grateful just for a quiet night—I was sick of being grateful for things that we had always taken for granted. I was sick of my own high exalted level, this climbing up onto a cloud, a dimension out of time. I hated the thought of *Abide with me.* Though indeed, indeed—the trite old words of the familiar, long-forgotten hymn tunes had come true. What had I known of the *darkness deepens* when I sang to my grandmother? I had sung those words as an inquisitive, sensitive, overstrung, possibly undernourished child, and now that I was overstrung, undernourished, it all came back.

I had gone round and round, and now I had made the full circle, now I had come back to the beginning. But the words of the hymns were trite, were trivial, and the net of the fowler was no longer a neat Asiatic metaphor but an actuality. *But it shall not come nigh thee* at this moment was almost a displeasing thought, for sometimes when the mind reaches its high peak of endurance, there is almost the hope—God forgive us—that the bomb that must fall on someone, would fall on me—but it could not—it must not. Because if the bomb fell on me, it would fall on Bryher, and Bryher must go on. That is the way we are trapped, that is the way I was trapped.

Bryher was my special heritage as I had been hers, but she would go on. She did not need me as she had at the end of the last war, and the child was grown up. . . .

Bryher said again, "It's the second wave."

Yes, we were drowning again. We had had almost a hundred air raids in succession in the worst days; that was after the Battle of Britain and we had recovered and now the tide-wave of terror swept over us again. We were drowning again.

The second wave! We would go down, we had gone down, the wave was breaking over us and if we came up to the surface again, there was only one certainty; there would be the third wave. Would the third wave be the last wave? It is true that the psyche, the soul can endure anything. But one did not want the body broken—we must not think about that. I am sitting in the hall in one of the little chairs. Actually, we can breathe, we can talk.

"It's not just this raid," I said, "it's remembering all the others."

The terrific shattering reverberations of the great guns slackened for a moment. There seemed to be less shaking and rumbling and an echo as of thunderstorm, further off, was probably distant guns following the flight of the bombers that had already passed over our heads. The surprising thing was that we hadn't all gone raving mad; I do not believe actually one of our friends had left town, driven out by fear. We had had a few weekends and the short summer breaks but actually had scarcely missed less than a half-dozen of the near-hundred continuous days and nights of bombing, not to mention the later, still terrific, but less sustained attacks.

Bells clanged, an air raid warden shouted "Are you all right in there," someone in a pause called in the hush, "Puss-puss-puss-puss." Somebody's cat would or would not respond from behind a familiar ash can or an unfamiliar heap of smouldering bricks and mortar. It had been worthwhile. It had been worthwhile to prove to oneself that one's mind and body could endure the very worst that life had to offer—to endure—to be able to face this worst of all trials, to be driven down and down to the uttermost depth of subconscious terror and to be able to rise again.

"Well, then, it's nearly over," I said.

My hands were cold with that freezing uncanny cold-ness that one associates with ghosts and ghost stories and sitting in a circle in the dark when they told the story of the man who died of fright because he had nailed his coat to a coffin and thought a skeleton hand had got him. That was a delicious tremor of expectancy, at a party sitting in a circle in the dark. Well, hadn't this been a sort of party on a grand scale, on, you might say, almost a cosmic scale?

Being shut up in a cupboard in the dark was really associated with games of hide-and-seek and the skeleton hand of death was something to be scared of at a party and to watch other people being scared of, afterwards at the next party. Going down and down in the dark was a sensation to be watched, to be enjoyed even if I had touched rock bot-tom. I had gone down under the wave and I was still alive, I was breathing. I was not drowning though in a sense, I had drowned; I had gone down, been submerged by the wave of memories and terrors repressed since the age of ten and long before, but with the terrors, I had found the joys, too.

On the opposite wall, the mirror was still set at its cor-rect angle. It was a smallish square of glass set in a wide frame of Neapolitan or Pompeian inlaid wood of different colors. It was set square and solid against the wall and we had not thought it necessary to take it down when we put away the china and had the glass over the doors blocked in. The mirror frame did not budge, although there was a slightly different pitch or tone to the new reverberations.

"I don't know whether they're flying higher or lower or whether it's them or whether it's us," I said.

"It's not us," Bryher said, though my remark had not

required an answer. But even if she had not answered it, it would have been immediately answered by the short, staccato perfectly measured beat of a new utterance.

"I don't know where that comes from." I said. "I thought we knew all the gun positions."

"It must be a mobile gun," she said.

"Yes," I said.

"Anyway, it's the third wave," she said.

But I was not afraid. The noise was outside. Death was outside. The terror had a name. It was not inchoate, unformed. *Wunden Eiland?* Was that this island, England, pock-marked with formidable craters, with Death stalking one at every corner?

It is very quiet. My knees are trembling and I am so cold. I am terribly cold, but though my knees are trembling, I seem to be sitting here motionless, not frozen into another dimension but here in time, in clock-time. "I wonder what time it is," I say to Bryher. "It wasn't a very long raid," I say to Bryher, "I wish we could talk to someone."

They told us that gravity or something of that sort would keep the stars from falling. But their wisdom and their detachment hadn't kept the stars from falling. The bombers had gone now, but the reaction after the prolonged battle is sometimes more shattering than the raids themselves. But the terror and the tension and the disassociation must come to an end sometimes.

Bryher is standing in the door. We will open all the doors now, and I will, with an effort, get out of this chair and stagger into the kitchen and fill a kettle and strike a match and arrange a tea tray.

"I'll get tea now," I say. . . .

I push open the kitchen door and turn round. I stand by the kitchen door opposite the mirror, *in a glass darkly*. But now face to face. We have been face to face with the final realities. We have been shaken out of our ordinary dimension in time and we have crossed the chasm that divides time from time-out-of-time or from what they call eternity.

I heard Christian Renatus saying:

> *Wound of Christ,*
> *Wound of God,*
> *Wound of Beauty,*
> *Wound of Blessing,*
> *Wound of Poverty,*
> *Wound of Peace*

and it went on and on, while underneath it there was the deep bee-like humming of the choir of Single Brothers and then the deeper sustained bass note that must have been Christian David who had a voice like my great-grandfather who made clocks and kept bees and was called *princeps facile* of musicians. *Princeps facile* they called him in Latin and then there was another language about passing the tomb. *L'amitié passe même le tombeau,* that was; that was French and it was the motto on the seal that the old great-great uncle had, and it was the writing at the head of the parchment that my other grandfather, Christian Henry Seidel, found.

L'amitié passe même le tombeau.

Now Golden Eagle with his arrows, has driven off the enemy; it is a cry and it is a liturgy, the litany of the wounds; pity us, sings Christian David deep deep down so that the even flow of the subdued bee-like humming of the choir of Single Brothers seems like a swarm of bees around the deep bell ringing, ringing in Christian David's throat; pity us, he says every time that the young Count Christian Renatus pronounces another one of his single strophes of his liturgy of the wounds. Our earth is a wounded island as we swing round the sun.

Harken to us, sings the great choir of the strange voices that speak in a strange bird-like staccato rhythm, but I know what they are saying though they are speaking Indian dialects. The two voices answer one another and the sound of Anna von Pahlen's voice as she reads the writing on the strip of paper from the woven basket that Cammerhof has just handed her, is pure and silver and clear like a silver trumpet.

I will give him the Morning Star reads Anna, and the head of the Indian priests, who is Shooting Star, later to be baptized Philippus, answers in his own language, *Kehelle* and then Hail, and they call together to the Great Spirit and the Good Spirit who is the God of the Brotherhood and the God of the Initiates. . . .

. . . it comes nearer, it is the shouting of many horsemen, it is Philippus, Lover-of-horses, it is Anna, Hannah or Grace, who is answering. Now they call together in one voice . . . the sound accumulates, gathers sound . . . "It's the all-clear," says Bryher. "Yes," I say.

London
1941
1943